# DEDICATION

D1362893

This book is dedicated first and foremost to ...,

He has been my biggest fan since we met in 1995 and I really couldn't have done anything I have achieved in life without him.

He is always on my side, no matter what.

I feel incredibly lucky to share my life with him and he makes me laugh every day.

Not only is he a great husband and my very best friend, David is also a wonderful father to our two fabulous children Charlie and Daisy.

I told Charlie and Daisy I was writing this book when I just started and this motivated me to get it finished.

Because they are the last two people on earth I would want to let down.

Thanks also to the brilliant Dave Trott for letting me use his incredible Bill Shankly story in the "If It's to be, it's up to me" chapter. I have read and loved every single one of Dave Trott's books. And thanks to Dave's daughter Jade for the fantastic book cover design.

I also have to thank Donna Orender, CEO of Orender Unlimited for inviting me along to talk at her fantastic Generation W conference, as it was at this conference where CNN's Kelly Wallace encouraged me to write the book. Thank you Donna and thank you Kelly. I did it. And whatever you want to do, you can do it too.

# Win Your Lottery

## - My ten simple steps to be as happy and as rich as you want to be

## By Sharry Cramond

This book is for everyone who wants to win the lottery.

ISBN: 978-1-5272-7152-4

# CONTENTS

# INTRODUCTION

Something happened to me when I was eleven years old that changed my life.

When I was eleven, I started "big" school – 'high school' as it's called in Scotland.

At this school you had to wear the school uniform.

But my family could not really afford to just go out and buy a brand new school uniform.

So, I went with my mum round the second hand shops and, success, we found the blazer for the school.

On the first day of school, I went round to my friend's house and knocked the door.

When she answered, she looked at my blazer and the first thing she said was "oh, do you know you are in the wrong colour?"

What me and my mum didn't know was that a few years back the school had changed the blazer.

Still blue, but a different shade of blue, and different material too.

In that moment, I felt like bursting into tears and running home crying.

But I knew that would ruin my day and would also ruin my mum's day.

I don't know where I got it from, but I said right back to my friend "yes, I do know that I am in the wrong colour...

...but I actually prefer this colour"

"Oh", said my friend, accepting my answer.

She must have thought that I had seen both the old style blazer and the new blazer and had simply decided that I liked this one best.

And that rather than following everyone else like sheep, I had made my own decision on which blazer to wear.

On that first day of school, I felt as though all 300 pupils who were starting "big" school that day all said to me "do you know you are in the wrong colour" and to each and every one of them I replied "yes, I do know.  But I actually prefer this colour".

And they all accepted my answer.

When I was walking home from school at the end of the day I thought to myself what a good day I had had.

I looked down at my blazer and thought "do you know what, I actually DO prefer this colour!"

I learned three things about myself that day that stuck with me for life:

1. That if you can tell yourself something over and over, it can become your truth (this works on the positive as well as the negative by the way)

2. That's it's nice to be nice (although my friend was actually a lovely girl, I am not sure that if I had been her that the first thing I would have said was "do you know you are in the wrong colour?")

3. That's it's OK to be different. In fact, it's GOOD to be different. (More about that later)

It fascinated me that I had gone from being horrified at being in the "wrong" colour to actually and genuinely preferring that colour, just by saying "I prefer this colour" over and over and over and over as everyone questioned me.

Just by thinking differently, I actually *felt* different.

Just by thinking differently, I actually *was* different.

For the rest of my childhood and into early adulthood, I spent years reading every book on the power of the mind and listening to every motivational audio book course I could get my hands on to try to understand how just thinking differently could be so powerful.

And I have read so many autobiographies of successful people to try to understand how some people are successful and some people are not.

I learned so much from all my reading.

And I learned that most things were possible if you just decided to choose to start thinking and acting differently.

Although I was never academically the smartest in school, I went on to have a hugely successful career as a Marketing Executive, working all over the world.

Do you ever look around you and wonder why some people seem to get on in life and some don't - and it's not always those who are the smartest that get on?

I realised this very early on.

I understood that success was 90% attitude and 10% ability.

Millions of people in this country have one big dream - to win the lottery.

Because that's their way out of their current situation.

That's their way out of poverty, that's how they will change their life.

I am passionate about showing them and others that there is another way.

Now there's nothing wrong with playing the lottery, but play for fun.

Don't base your dreams on it.

I want to show how you can win YOUR OWN lottery.

Simply by thinking and acting differently.

When I was in the US, I was speaking at the brilliant Generation W ('W' stands for women) conference in Jacksonville, Florida.

I was sharing some of the tips I had picked up on how you can start thinking differently and changing your life.

The audience seemed to like it and in fact, Donna Orender, the CEO of the organising company, said I was one of the most mentioned speakers in the follow up research.

One of the other speakers was Kelly Wallace, a digital correspondent for CNN at the time.

I was a bit in awe of Kelly - I mean she worked for CNN!

In the green room afterwards, where the presenters were

hanging out, Kelly said she loved what I said.

She said I should write all my learnings into a book.

In fact she said more than that - Kelly said:

*"I've been to plenty of women's conferences and heard many a keynote from women hoping to motivate their audiences but I don't know if I've ever heard a presentation as inspiring, relatable, funny and authentic as Sharry Cramond's during the Generation W annual conference in Jacksonville, Florida this spring.*

*In between cracking up with laughter, I found myself taking copious notes about Sharry's life lessons, which I know will help me in whatever journey I pursue in the future.*

*Her story, which was so beautifully described starting with the experience of being the only 11-year-old to wear the wrong color blazer to school, speaks to women of all ages, stages and educational and economic backgrounds. She went from nothing to being named one of the top 100 marketers in the world. You can think differently, you can change your life, you can be whatever you want to be, she said. And I bet every woman in that audience walked away from her speech thinking they could do the same.*

*Using humor and honesty, Sharry connects with the audience in an 'I'm just like you' way. That relatability combined with her decades of experience in leading and motivating employees makes her a real star in the lifting up women movement. Her book aptly titled "Win Your Lottery" would no doubt be a hit with women and men who can learn from Sharry's story and make changes in their own lives -- no matter their income or educational level.*

*And that's really what sets Sharry's story apart from so many of the other self-help books that often target white-collar professionals. Sharry's story and book are for everyone.*

*I wholeheartedly endorse a book by Sharry Cramond and believe there is nothing comparable available to readers at this time.*

So thank you Donna and thank you Kelly.

I wrote the book.

From everything I have learned, I wrote a book explaining my ten simple tips to changing your life and helping you achieve the success you want.

But unlike all the other self help books out there, I believe this book is very different.

This isn't just written for professional, office-based, business leaders - with long words, complex theories and thousands of pages.

This book is written for everyday people.

It's written for people who may never even have heard of the 'self help' genre before.

I haven't found that anyone else had written self help books for this population, but yet they were the ones who needed it the most.

I called my book WIN YOUR LOTTERY.

And in my ten simple chapters, I would show how you could.

I deliberately kept the book simple.

And short.

Someone once told me "when you give advice, be concise".

So I haven't waffled on for pages and pages just so I could be proud of my big thick book with lots of pages.

I really wanted this book to appeal to all those people who have never picked up a motivational book before and dismissed all this stuff as "mumbo jumbo" or just simply "not for them".

Or they may not have even known that books like this existed?

Every positivity book I've read seems to have been created for the middle classes, with lots of examples from the "boardroom" or when "leading teams".

I wanted to write a book that works for everyone.

Whether you are a nurse, a teacher, an electrician or currently unemployed.

Not a big thick tome that is full of big words (in my experience, big words are usually used to disguise a lot of bulsh*t").

But a simple, easy to follow book full of simple tips that REALLY WORK.

I wanted to show that if I could come from a council estate to a globally successful business executive, then quite frankly anyone can do it, as I am nothing special.

I wanted everyone to have access to these simple techniques.

Not just business leaders.

So everyone can win *their* lottery.

The lottery of life.

# 1 GOING THE EXTRA MILE

*Always go the extra mile, you'll find it's never crowded.*

Imagine that your boss called all of his or her employees together on Monday morning and announced that you would all be having a tiny video camera installed on your shoulder for that week and that this video camera would record everything you said or did for a week in the hours that you were at work.

If you are self employed, let's say you are a plumber, then imagine that someone from your trade association gathered all the plumbers in your city together and said the same thing.

And that at the end of that week he or she would be reviewing all the videos and that the person who had worked the hardest at the end of that week would receive one million pounds cash there and then.

By hardest, they don't mean the person who worked the longest hours.

They simply mean the person that, for the hours they were at work, were fully present and focused and really tried their best.

They didn't sit in meetings and daydream.

Even for a second.

They didn't let their minds wander onto what was for dinner that night or what they were doing at the weekend.

They remained 100% focused on the job in hand.

They didn't keep looking at their watch to see when it was hometime.

Instead they enjoyed every hour and every minute they were working.

They didn't stop for numerous coffee breaks during the day.

They didn't check their Facebook every hour.

Instead, they made the most of every second they were being paid to work.

They put in the maximum effort every second of every day.

If they were a teacher, they made sure every single lesson was engaging and informative.

If they were a retail worker, they had a smile for every customer and treated them with as much respect as they possibly could.

If they were a plumber, they worked efficiently and had a smile for the customer.

In fact, they finished the job early and surprised the customer by saying that the job actually took less time and cost less than they thought.

If they were a mum they didn't spend half the day on social media - they focused on their child or their home and did their very best.

If they were a student at school or college they vowed to learn and focus and listen better than they ever had done before.

They actively participated in every class and asked questions to make sure they really understood.

I could go on and on.

When I have spoken about this at conferences and asked the audience to raise their hands if they would act differently if they had a mini video camera installed for a week and the chance to compete for a million pounds cash - *every single hand in the room went up.*

Every single person said they would act differently at work, school or college that week if that were the case.

If this incentive was on offer.

Who wouldn't right?

Who wouldn't put in the most effort or work harder and smarter and be more focused than they ever had done in their life.

Who wouldn't smile and engage more with their clients, their boss, their students, their workmates, if it meant they had a chance to get that million pounds.

Every single person said they would work harder and be more focused that week than they had ever done in their life.

They had to be better than everyone else right.

And if smiling and exuding happiness and a good attitude in the workplace was part of the criteria to win, then my goodness they would have the biggest smile on their faces and be the most pleasant and well-liked person that anyone would dream to have around them.

My gosh they were going to outwork everyone else.

Out-smile everyone else.

Be more focused than everyone else.

Work harder and smarter than everyone else.

Be nicer than everyone else.

Come up with more ideas than everyone else.

Finish work quicker than everyone else and surprise their boss by asking for more to do.

They were literally going to be the model employee or student for that week.

They were 100% focused on winning that one million pound cash prize.

Well, I have news for you.

If you want to get on, **be like that now**.

Be like that every day.

Many people want to know the 'secret to success' and the secrets to getting on in life.

Be. Like. That. Now.

Work and act and be as though you had a hidden video camera on your shoulder and you were being assessed for a weekly one million pound cash prize.

Because quite simply, that is the way to get on.

It sounds ludicrously simple, but I can assure you **most people don't act like this**.

You will stand out from the crowd like a beacon.

And one day it **could** lead you to a million pound pay packet!

I heard of a man who left school and started working as a toilet cleaner for a fast food chain.

Now I can't think of many jobs I would rather do less than being a toilet cleaner at a fast food chain.

But he decided that if he had to clean toilets then he may as well be the best toilet cleaner they had ever had.

He worked faster than all the other toilet cleaners.

He made sure the toilets were the cleanest they had ever been.

And he did all of it with a smile on his face for his co-workers.

So he stood out from all the other toilet cleaners, of course.

And then he was then promoted to making burgers.

Again, he decided that if he was going to be making burgers, he was going to be the best burger-maker they had ever had.

And as always, all done with a huge smile and a positive and warm personality.

He stuck with this attitude and was promoted and promoted until he had a huge leadership role at the organization.

All because he always went the extra mile.

If you are a plumber who acts like this, do you think that every single client of yours will tell all their friends and family what an absolutely amazing plumber they had found.

And if you finished earlier, and did the job better and then charged them less than everyone else as it didn't take as long as you thought (as you didn't waste time on your phone or going for long coffee breaks) don't you think that would make you stand out from the crowd.

If you work in retail and you smile all day regardless of how tired you are and nothing is too much for you to do and you treat every customer as though they were a world leader or a famous celebrity, do you think that would make you different from others?

If you work in an office as part of a team and you are always the first person to raise your hand when the boss is looking for someone to volunteer to organize the team day or some other task that's not really part of anyone's job description, do you think that would make you more of an ideal employee?

As a leader of people myself, I cannot tell you how much of a difference this can make by the way.

Some people think that getting on in life is pretty much based on your abilities.

Let's say, 90% on your ability and 10% on your attitude.

Some even say it's more like 50/50.

Getting on in life, I believe, is 90% attitude and just 10% ability.

So it's not about, oh so-and-so is smarter than me, had better opportunities than me.

That's just excuses.

I have generally found that there is very little difference in people in terms of ability.

I interview lots of people and by the time I interview them they have already been assessed by human resources and others.

So by the time I see the short list of candidates they all have the **ability** to do the job.

So what makes me pick one person over another when they are all pretty much, on paper anyway, similar?

The difference that makes people stand out is their attitude.

And it can make a BIG difference whether it is positive or

negative.

Everyone wants to work with "can do" rather than "it's always a problem" people.

Do you every look around you at work and wonder why some people get on and some people don't?

And it's not always the smartest people who get on, right.

But it usually is the people with the best attitudes who get on.

Choose to be positive and always go the extra mile.

In my experience, this definitely gives you the best chance of success.

*Because hardly anyone else acts like this.*

They just don't.

If every single person put up their hands when asked if they would act differently if there was a one million cash prize on the table at the end of the week, then every single person is not giving a 100% effort to what they are doing right now.

Be that person who always gives 100% right now.

Act like that right now.

Every single time you find yourself daydreaming in a meeting, get right back to work.

Back on it.

Focus.

Contribute.

And smile.

Be enthusiastic.

Don't waste time.

Always think of what you can do better.

Did I say smile.

Be a pleasant person to be around.  (This is so important).

Can you think of someone you work with who is always miserable.

Always moaning.

How are you today?

"Oh, not too bad", they moan, and then proceed to tell you what's so bad about their life.

People love to moan, don't they?

Well, number one, don't be that moaning person.

And number two, don't waste time listening to that moaning.

There are two different types of people – radiators and drains.

Radiator-type people radiate energy and positivity.

Whereas drains sap everyone around them of all of their energy, with their constant negativity.

Don't be a drain – be a radiator!

Focus on what you are doing.

And if someone asks how you are, just say "fabulous".

And then get back to work.

Always, always go the extra mile.

Not only will you find it's never crowded, you will actually find there's practically no-one else there.

Just by adopting this new attitude you will stand out from the crowd in a good way.

Try it for a month.

If that's too hard (come on, it so isn't) then try it for a week.

For a whole week convince yourself that you are all being assessed for that one million pounds cash prize.

Become the employee of the week.

The employee of the month, the year.

Make it your business to be the hardest working and most pleasant employee in your whole company.

If you are self employed then become the most pleasant and hard working and focused and best value person in your profession.

Be the happiest most dedicated teacher in your school, in the whole country!

Always, always, always go the extra mile.

People will want to work with you.

They will want you on their team.

People will want to work **for** you.

People will recommend you.

You will be more successful than ever before.

I absolutely guarantee you that this works.

What have you got to lose.

You have to be in work or working between the hours of xx and yy anyway.

So you may as well give this a go while you are there.

You have nothing to lose and while you may not get a million pounds cash in a week, you will get on and get more customers, more promotions, more pay rises than ever before.

Wherever you go, or whatever you do, put your heart and soul into it every day.

From a toilet cleaner to a corporate executive, this stuff works.

Do more than you are paid for now and eventually you will be paid more.

Don't count every hour.

Instead, make every hour count.

Act like you have that invisible video camera on your shoulder every day.

# 2 YOU HAVE GOT TO HAVE GOALS

*If you haven't got a goal, how can you score?*

I heard a story of a graduating class at university who were all asked if they had goals and if they had them written down.

Only 1% of the class had written goals.

Twenty years later, all of the class were interviewed again and they found that the 1% who had written goals were happier and wealthier than the other 99% added together.

I wonder then if the 99% of the population with no goals spend all their time helping the 1% achieve theirs?

Have you ever set a New Year's Resolution?

A survey found that only 4% of people ever keep theirs.

But of those who actually wrote down their Resolutions, 44% kept them.

Writing down your goals or Resolutions takes, like, five minutes.

When I heard this it really made me stop and think.

Wow.

Just by writing down what I wanted I would have more chance of achieving it?

Daft not to then isn't it?

The more I have thought about and learned about goals, the more convinced I am that this is one of the absolute keys to success.

Imagine a little sailboat sailing across the ocean.

When a storm comes, the sailboat gets spun around, backwards and forwards and side to side.

But when the storm goes away and everything is calm again, the sailboat gets itself back into the right direction and carries on until it reaches it's destination.

Now if you imagine that you are that sailboat, sailing through life.

When stormy times come (and we all have stormy times in life from time to time) we get spun around and knocked out of shape – we don't know whether we are coming or going.

But when life gets back to normal again, we get ourselves back on track, back in the direction of our goals.

But if we don't have a goal and we don't have a clear direction of travel, then we just wait until the stormy times have passed and then we just keep going in whatever direction we end up facing.

Be that left, right, or even backwards!

It's a bit like using google maps for directions.

When they hit a roadblock, or we take a wrong turn, they find another route to get around the obstacle, but to still get to the right final destination.

If you didn't have a final destination programmed in, then you would just go in whatever direction the roadblock took you.

People with goals are not just go-getters, they are goal-getters!

They are focused and driven.

They know where they want to get to.

Albert Einstein said "Life is like riding a bicycle. To keep your balance, you must keep moving"

People without goals aren't moving – they are drifters.

They have no goals (just dreams, like winning the lottery) and no real commitment to achieving anything.

They blame others or their upbringing ("my parents didn't understand me blah blah blah")

They do the bare minimum so they don't get fired.

And they never do anything to improve their situation.

We *have* to have a final destination in mind, a goal.

And we *have* to have it programmed into our brain.

We have to have a goal to give us a direction of travel.

How can we hit a target when we don't even know where it is?

When I first starting thinking of goals, I wrote down that I wanted to have a car – specifically a Golf GTI.

Do you know I then started seeing them everywhere.

Have you ever experienced that?

You decide you want to get brand xx of a car and suddenly you see them everywhere?

It was weird.

Why suddenly is everyone driving a Golf GTI?

But they were not "suddenly" driving them.

They were always there.

I just hadn't noticed them before.

And that's a bit like seeing opportunities to achieve your goals.

If you have a goal, suddenly, as though it's a coincidence, people and opportunities will come into your life that help you achieve your goal.

But it's not a coincidence.

Your mind is simply programmed to look for these opportunities.

So it's much easier to spot them.

Just like with the Golf cars.

They were always there.

But unless you are focused on them, you just won't notice.

And so many great opportunities may just pass you by.

So you have got to have goals and you have got to have them written down.

How hard can this be?

Whatever busy job you have or even if you are currently unemployed, it can't be that difficult to get a hold of a pen and a piece of paper.

## Getting started on writing your goals

To get you started, think of things you want to achieve.

Simple things, like stopping biting your nails, being fitter, thinner...whatever it is that you want.

(We will come on to career goals in a minute).

Here's the key though.

Write down the goal as if it has already been achieved.

So instead of "I want to stop biting my nails" you would say "I have beautiful long nails".

Instead of "I want to lose weight" you would say "I weigh xx pounds".

Instead of "I want to do more exercise" you may say "I am running 5 miles every day" or whatever you think could be achievable in the future.

You may think this sounds mad – how can it be a goal when you are writing it down as though it has already been achieved.

I am not going to bore you too much with the power of the mind or how the brain works.

But let me simply say that if you implant these statements into your sub-conscious mind as though they are **already** true then an amazing thing starts happening.

Your subconscious mind **believes** these statements, as you put them in there as statements of fact.

Your subconscious is what some people say is your "right" side of your brain.

The right side of your brain is your creative side.

It's where your imagination sits.

When you dream at night, that's coming from your subconscious mind.

To get a goal into your subconscious mind you have to imagine it in your head as though it is already true.

Let's take the nails as an example.

Cut out a colour picture from a magazine of some beautiful nails and stick them underneath your written goal.

Now close your eyes and totally relax.

The best time is lying in bed at night when it's really quiet and you can concentrate.

In your mind, see yourself looking at your nails, painted

bright red or another bright color.

Smell the nail polish.

Hear people commenting on how beautiful your nails are.

The more vividly you can imagine this, the more implanted into your subconscious mind it will go.

The right brain is the sensory side of your brain.

It thinks in colour.  It helps with the sense of smell.

So really bring the goal alive with all the senses in your head.

OK, so now the goal is implanted into your subconscious.

But you have to keep it going.

Do this literally every night.

Keep imagining, in vivid color, your goal as though you had already achieved it.

Now on the left side of your brain is your logical side.

That's the side that works out maths equations or simple everyday things like speaking.

When the  logical left side of your brain sees the goal in your subconscious it says, hold on.

That's not right.

My nails are not like that.

But the subconscious mind believes it to be true as it cannot differentiate what you have simply implanted there and what it has seen in reality.

What you have created is an imbalance in your brain between the subconscious and the conscious.

And the brain does not like imbalance.

So it gets to work to bring things back to balance.

You know when you are queuing up behind someone and they have a big piece of fluff on their back and you just want to pick it off?

Or if you were sitting in a doctor's waiting room and someone scrunched up a piece of paper and threw it into the middle of the room and you would keep looking at it and want to pick it up and put it in the bin.

Well that's because your logical conscious mind likes everything to be in balance and "just right".

So you can imagine how much it does not like the new "fact" that is sitting in the subconscious mind!

What happens then is that your brain subconsciously gets to work to bring about the balance.

And it helps your willpower to stop biting your nails and grow them nice and long so you can paint them red, just like you imagined you were already doing.

Right now I am sure I have just about lost some of you.

Bear with me, please.

When I first heard this stuff I honestly thought it sounded either (a) like a load of old rubbish or (b) like some kind of weird magic

It's not.

It really, really works.

Hypnotizing works right?

We have all seen world famous hypnotists, either on TV or maybe even in person.

Well, this works too.

Just try it.

What have you got to lose?

Nothing.

And what have you got to gain?

The achievement of your goals for one.

To have what you really want in life.

I was totally sceptical about all this, but do you know what, I tried it and it worked.

And not just for me, for so many people.

Almost every successful person I have read about does this.

So please, get started.

1. Write down your goals as though you have already achieved them

2. Cut out colour pictures and stick them underneath your written goal (the more vivid the better)

3. Look at your goal every day

4. Imagine your goal in your mind in vivid detail, as though it has already happened

Now I said I would come back to career goals.

For lots of people, they are really clear with what they want for their career goals.

A builder may say "I have my own building contracting business and I employ ten builders and have a turnover of xxx per year"

A teacher may say "I am headteacher at a secondary school in Cornwall" (the more specific you can be in your goals the better by the way)

But some people just don't know what they want to do.

All they know if that they don't like their current job.

(Remember what we learned in the first chapter though – right now you have to be there so you may as well put everything into it in the hours that you are there)

So make it your goal to know what you want to do by a specific date.

For example your goal would be "I know exactly what career is right for me by xx date" and they see themselves bouncing out of bed in the morning and happily going to work and they see themselves coming home at night and talking about what an amazing day they had at work.

And OK they don't know yet what the bit in the middle is, but it's their goal to work it out.

And just like with any goals, the mind gets to work to help

you achieve it.

People and situations will "coincidentally" come into your life to help you find the right answer.

Just like the Golf GTIs "suddenly" appeared.

## Helping Your Goals Come True

Many of you may have read about the importance of goal setting before and are thinking, so what am I actually learning different here?

So here are a few tips I have for really helping you make those goals come true.

Number one, write your goal on a small piece of paper (again, as though it is already true) then give that paper to someone you trust and respect.

Tell them what it is and ask them to keep it in their wallet.

You now know that every time that person opens their wallet they will see your goal.

And you know that they are sure to be wondering how you are getting on with achieving it.

I did this when I was working in Australia.

I was moving back to the UK to do a global marketing role.

It was a great job, but would involve lots of travel.

The job I really wanted was in the company's UK Marketing team.

So I wrote on a small scrap of paper "Sharry Cramond is Marketing Director in the UK Marketing team" and I asked a colleague in Australia who I really respected to put this piece of paper in her wallet.

Where I knew she would see it every day.

And every day she looked at it and I *wasn't* working in the UK Marketing team, she would know that I hadn't yet achieved my goal.

And because I cared what she thought of me, it really spurred me on to achieve that goal.

And do you know what, after just a year in the global role I was working as Marketing Director in the UK Marketing team

If your goal was that you had beautiful nails, and you wrote this on a piece of paper and gave it to someone whose opinion you cared about, then you know that they would look at your nails every time they saw you.

And if they were still bitten to the core they would notice.

And you would notice them noticing.

If your goal was that you weighed twenty pounds less than you weigh now, then you know that when they see you they will look at you to see how you are getting on.

If they saw you eating a chocolate bar after they had just that morning read your goal of weight loss in their wallet, then they might wonder whether you were really committed to your goal.

If your goal was that you were running an upcoming

marathon then they would be wondering how much training you were doing.

That extra bit of pressure spurs you on to achieve your goal.

Next, tell everyone about your goal.

Some people say you should keep your goal to yourself.

I completely disagree.

If you tell everyone at work that you are committed to weighing 20 pounds less, do you really think you are going to feel comfortable eating a chocolate bar at your desk?

You might *want* to eat the chocolate bar at your desk, but you are much more likely *not* to as everyone knows your goal.

When I decided to write this book I told my kids that I was writing it and that it would be finished by Christmas.

They were really proud of me.

Wow.

An actual book written by our actual mum.

They thought this would be just amazing.

And they totally believed that it would be happening.

My son asked could he get a signed copy for his teacher.

My daughter said could I mention her in the dedication at the end of the book.

They asked me every day how many pages I had written

and when would it be finished and published and they would have a printed copy. (Children are not known for their patience)

Do you think that spurred me on to write it even faster, even when I was tired from my full time hectic job?

Absolutely it did.

I couldn't let me kids down, could I.

So tell everyone your goals.

And if you have kids, tell them too.

In fact, tell them first.

Next, write a letter to yourself as though your goal is already achieved, congratulating yourself.

Write the letter and post it.

Do this every week or at least every month until you have achieved this goal.

For example, "Dear Sharry. I am so proud of you that you are going out running three times a week.

You are so much fitter.

And that 5 mile run you completed was just amazing.

Well done.

Love from Sharry. X"

Now I know.

It sounds daft right.

I mean writing a letter to yourself.

Really.

Again, it's the cost of a stamp and an envelope.

What have you got to lose?

Nothing.  What have you got to gain?

The achievement of your goal.

Finally, record a video of yourself on your phone talking about your goal as thought it has already been achieved.

Be so excited and delighted that you have achieved this goal.

Be completely as over the top happy as you want.

Only you have to see this video so really go for it!

Now watch the video every day.

And at least twice a day if you can.

First thing in the morning and last thing at night.

When you hear yourself and the absolute pleasure the version of you in the video is getting from that goal being achieved, again it just helps spur you on.

You can't let yourself down, right.

Try all or any of these tips.

They work.

Please give it a go.

When you motivate your brain it goes after it.

Become a goal seeking missile.

# 3 HAPPY TALK

You know those days when you wake up in the morning and oversleep your alarm and then everything seems to go wrong the whole day?

We have all been there.

And what do most people say when this is happening?

"I am having a bad day"

I **am having** a bad day.

It's like you are saying it as a statement of intention.

Like, I am having chinese take-out tonight.

I **am having** a bad day.

They tell themselves this and, guess what, they do have a bad day.

Because they are telling themselves, in fact, **instructing** themselves, to have a bad day.

Think of when you are trapped in a traffic jam.

Now, unless you can transport yourself into space, you are pretty much stuck in that traffic jam.

So you have two choices.

You can either get really annoyed.

Thump the steering wheel.

Shout and swear.

But will that get you out of the traffic jam?

Will that help your situation?

Will that change your situation?

Of course it won't.

You will still be stuck in the traffic jam.

What if instead you said "fantastic - gives me time to phone my mum" or "great - I get some quiet time just to think; some time just for me"

Or you simply smile and enjoy some time listening to the radio.

(Or better still, an audio course!)

Which option do you think would put you in a better mood for the day??

Now you may think, hold on - being stuck in a traffic jam is super annoying.

How can I possibly smile and think happy thoughts.

But we all DO have the ability to control how we respond to

a situation.

You know the word "responsibility".

Try splitting this word up.

Response.

Ability.

We all have the **ability** to choose our **response**.

To choose whether to be happy or to be annoyed.

Just tell yourself "great – I have some time to myself"

Say it out loud.

You are stuck in the traffic jam whether you like it or not.

So why let it spoil your day.

Don't just act.

Think.

It's a bit like going to work every day.

Unless you are already a multi-millionaire, we all have to work right.

So between the hours of xx and yy, we have to be at work.

We can choose to be miserable at work and clock watch all day, waiting for home time.

We can choose to moan and groan all day about how much you don't want to be there.

About how hard Mondays are.

And Tuesdays.

In fact every day.

Thank goodness it's Friday.

Survived another week.

Or we can choose to be happy at work.

To smile at colleagues, customers, clients and students.

Again, which option do you think would give us a better day?

Choose to love what you do.

For the moment, you have to do it.

So choose to love it.

Simple as that.

Do you know when most people die of a heart attack?

You might not be surprised to learn that in fact it's Monday mornings.

They hate their job.

It's the start of another week.

They didn't win the lottery at the weekend.

Most people talk about happiness as something that will happen in the future and something that is dependent on certain criteria.

"I will be happy when I get xxxxx job"

"I will be happy when I earn £xxxxx"

"I would be really happy if I drove a xxxx car or lived in a house worth £xxxx"

They spend their whole life planning when they *will* be happy.

And then it's too late.

When it comes to work, really, you have two choices:-

1. Find a job you love
2. Love the job you have

Now of course you want to have a goal to find a great job in your dream field.

But I absolutely guarantee you that if you go for option 2 above, that will definitely help you achieve option 1!

I decided years ago that I was just going to choose to be happy

It actually was as simple as that.

I know it might sound ridiculous.

But it was really that easy.

I chose to be happy.

Sometimes I have to go away for work and I don't see my husband or children for a number of days.

I can choose to be annoyed and upset.

To go on all day about how I will miss everyone.

About how unfair it is.

But guess what, even with all my moaning, I still have to go on the business trip.

So it was pretty much a complete waste of time moaning.

Or I can choose to be happy.

To look forward to the trip.

To enjoy the trip.

To laugh with my colleagues.

To make the most of all the time I am away.

Which option do you think would mean I would have a more successful business trip.

And which option do you think would help me come home in a really positive mood to see my lovely family at the end of the week.

This is not rocket science.

It is so simple it's almost crazy.

But we all really do have a choice on how we respond to situations.

The clue is in the word: RESPONSE – <u>ABILITY</u>.

When we were living in the US, my children were starting back school after the summer holidays.

Charlie starting in 3<sup>rd</sup> grade, Daisy is going in to 2<sup>nd</sup> grade.

My son asked if I was going to be dropping them off AND

picking them up on their first day back.

My response was unfortunately neither.

I was going to New York very early in the morning so they would still be asleep when I left.

I was staying overnight in New York so I wouldn't see them in the evening to talk through their first day back at school.

And then I wouldn't be back the next day until after they had gone to sleep, so I wouldn't even be able to speak to them after their second day back at school.

Now whether that was the ideal situation or not, there was nothing I could do about it.

I had to go to New York.

I had to miss the time with the children.

So I could be totally miserable and moan about it to the children and my husband.

I could let it spoil my whole weekend beforehand.

Or I could just accept my plans for the week.

Have a great weekend and feel excited about my trip to New York.

And not cause a miserable atmosphere at home when the children were getting ready for back to school.

Response.

Ability.

You can guess which option I chose.

You know sometimes when you have been really upset or really angry and at the end of it you feel literally exhausted?

That's because negative emotions really do drain us.

Can you remember the last time you had a good old cry and then afterwards you felt absolutely exhausted?

Think about it as though we wake up every day with a fully recharged battery.

But every time we get angry or annoyed, it depletes some of the battery energy.

Every moan, sucks out more energy from the battery.

Every bit of frustration, every time you and a work colleague start bad-mouthing someone, some more energy goes from your battery.

How much energy do you think the battery would have left at the end of the day?

That's right – very, very little.

How many times at the end of a day do you get home, flop on the sofa and say "I'm done".

Just like the battery.

There's no charge left.

Nothing for your family.

And nothing for you.

So you eat your dinner, flop on the sofa, go to bed...and then do it all again the next day.

Instead, if you go through your whole day choosing not to be annoyed, not to get frustrated, smiling more, actually BEING happy...how much energy do you think you would have left at the end of the day then?

Just try this – there's no harm in trying it and you might just be amazed at the results.

But it's not that easy you might say.

My life is rubbish/boring and I feel not great to say the least.

I would just be fooling myself.

Well I say do exactly that.

Fool yourself.

*Fake it until you feel it.*

You know when people are feeling low they sit all hunched up as though to make themselves smaller.

But when they are happy they feel much lighter and walk taller.

Almost as though they have a spring in their step.

Well if feeling low = hunched up, and feeling happy = head held high, I wonder if it could also work the other way around?

What I mean is, if we just change our body language, could we help trick our minds into thinking we feel differently?

Fake it until we feel it.

If we walk tall, look up and smile, could that make us

actually feel better?

I do this and amazingly it actually works.

Just as being happy means you smile, making yourself smile helps you feel happier - the reverse is also true.

Just as 2+3 equals 5.   5 also equals 2+3.

Again, what do you have to lose.

Just try this and see if it works for you!

It was a bit like me with wearing the wrong colour of blazer on my first day of school.

At first when I said "yes, but I prefer this colour" I was definitely just faking it.

But as I said it over and over, very definitely, throughout the day when everyone asked me over and over if I knew I was in the wrong colour, I actually starting believing it.

I started *feeling* it.

And by the end of the day, I actually DID prefer that colour!

Fake it until you feel it.

Walk tall, smile and I almost guarantee you will feel happier.

Remember when we talked about goals in chapter two, and we said when you decided you wanted a car and you choose a specific model you wanted (eg a Golf) and then you started seeing that model of car everywhere.

Have you ever heard the phrase "Be careful what you wish

for".

Pretty much all of the many books I have read and studied on this subject basically all say that you get what you wish for.

Whatever is dominant in your thoughts.

Whatever you think about all the time, you move closer towards in your life.

And not even just what you "wish" for – you get what you think about.

Whether that's negative or positive.

The first few times I read this I thought surely this is just mumbo jumbo.

It can't be right that whatever you think about all the time comes into your life?

But then when I thought about getting a Golf car and I started seeing them everywhere it worked though??

And then when I read the autobiographies of lots of famous and successful people, they all had one thing in common.

They all said "they had *dreamed about this all their life*".

They had imagined it and dreamt of it and thought about it every single day.

They all said that they had imagined what they wanted all their life...until it came true.

Can you really afford to just dismiss this as "mumbo jumbo" when it's working for so many other people.

So many other *successful* people.

Just think for a moment, what if it is true.

What if you really do get what you think about.

You might not initially believe this but is it really worth the risk?

If you think – I am useless, I am tired, I will lose my job, no-one will love me, I am having a bad day...etc etc

What if it's really true that 'what you think about is what you get'.

Yikes.

That would mean I AM useless.

I WILL always be tired.

I AM going to lose my job.

I WILL NOT ever find someone to love me

And I will just have one bad day after another.

Doesn't sound great does it.

So just try instead thinking a bit more positively.

A bit happier thoughts.

Much better instead to think - I WILL learn how to do this.

I have so much energy.

I am doing so well at my job.

My life partner is on his/her way.

I am having a GREAT day.

Even, I prefer this colour of blazer.

Imagine, just imagine that all of this then came true!

Again, just TRY this.

And again, what have you got to lose?

If you get what you think about then make sure you think about good stuff!

I read a great quote from Henry Ford who created the Ford motor company.

He said "Whether you think you can, or you think you can't - you're right"

So if you think you CAN do something, then guess what, you are right.

You actually CAN.

Keep focusing on it and you CAN do it.

But if you think you CAN'T do something, then guess what, you are also right.

Keep telling yourself you can't do it and you won't be able to.

As I said, be careful what you wish for.

Happy thoughts = happy life.

Sounds too simple.

People often ask me how I stop the self doubt and

negativity sneaking in?

I am not saying that I don't occasionally have a more negative thought.

You know when you get an email you don't like or don't need, what do you do?

That's right.

You simply delete it.

Well whenever a negative though comes into your head, just say to yourself DELETE, and imagine yourself pressing the delete on your phone or computer.

And then just as with emails, you would then go on to read the next email.

In your mind, just move your thoughts on to something you DO want (like one of your goals)

The moment you start thinking about something negative, see yourself pressing delete and just move on to the next thought.

Delete, Delete.  Delete.

Until a more positive thought comes.

Keep doing it all day if you have to, to make sure your brain focuses on the stuff you DO want.

The happy stuff.

Think about what would make you happy.

Where would you work?

Where would you live?

What would you do each weekend?

Write it all down.

And the minute a negative thought comes into your head,
DELETE, DELETE, DELETE.

And move on to the next one.

A happy thought.

And a much happier life

My grandad was a miner.

He lived with my grandmother and their seven children in a
working class, small mining town in central Scotland.

He would get up at the crack of dawn every day and head
to the mines.

He would then go deep underground and spend ten hours
chipping the coal from the earth.

This job played havoc with his health and, when he was in
his late 60s, he developed emphysema.

The emphysema killed him in his seventies.

Do you think he complained about doing that job or about
how it affected him?

Well, every single day he went down those mines, and do
you know what he did?

It wasn't moaning to his fellow workers - he went down
there every day...whistling.

That's right, whistling.

Every single day.

Because he had to do the job to feed his family, and there were no other jobs in town.

So he just chose to be happy with the job he had.

He knew he had to do the job, so he could either go down the mines miserable every day (like most of the other miners), or he could go down the mines whistling.

Now I obviously don't know what job you are doing right now, but I am fairly confident that for most it's not as bad as the one my poor old grandad had.

But I do know that you can *choose* to be happy with whatever you are doing.

So *choose* to be happy right now, before it's too late.

A study proved that the majority of your job success is based on how happy you are.

It's called "The Happiness Advantage" (a brilliant book written by Shawn Achor)

So the majority of your success is not about how smart or how talented you are, but how happy you choose to be.

Not only do happy people live longer then, they also do better at work.

Every time I have something challenging on, say a really, *really* early meeting, I think about my lovely grandad, whistling as he went down those mines every day.

And I smile, I purse my lips, and I get whistling.

# 4 IT'S NICE TO BE NICE

Remember my blazer story.

And that one of the things I learned was it's nice to be nice.

Well that has really stayed with me throughout my life.

And it's incredible what a difference this has made.

Because I have always treated people well and with respect, regardless of whether they were the cleaner or the CEO, I was able to call on so many people around the world to help me with the launch of this book.

There's an amazing quote from a lady called Maya Angelou which is "I've learned that people will forget what you said, people will forget what you did…but people will never forget how you made them feel"

How true is this.

Think back to the times in your life when this is true.

Think how people made you FEEL.

And think how quickly you would respond to help them now.

I am guessing that how they made you feel will be a key driver of your decision on that.

I saws a great story online about a man going to work and when he got to his work car park and was about to go into a space, someone nipped into the space in front of him.

It was totally obvious that the first man was going into this space.

But the other chap just decided to take it anyway.

Then the first man said, excuse me, but I was about to park there.

And then the man stealing the space told the first guy to "f**k off"

Nice.

How do you think it made the first guy feel?

Not great I would imagine.

He must have used his mental "delete" a fair bit that morning.

He then had to drive round and find another space.

He didn't want to be late that day as he was interviewing an external candidate for a role in his team that morning.

So when he eventually got to his office, can you imagine how he felt when he saw the candidate he was interviewing and realized it was the man who had stolen the space and been so rude to him.

How do you think the interview went after that.

I always try to make everyone I interact with feel better after the interaction with me than before.

Try this.

Because you never know where people are going to turn up, do you.

I am sure you have heard of the saying that there is only "six degrees of separation" separating anyone on the planet from anyone else.

That's a bit too close for comfort to go around annoying everyone isn't it.

My mum always used to always say to me "whatever you give out in life, you get back double"

Part of me always thought it was a load of old rubbish.

But the other part of me thought, what if this IS true?

If there was even a tiny part of it that was true, I decided to give out good stuff.

As then I would get double good stuff back.

Because if I gave out negativity and bad vibes, I certainly didn't want that coming back to me in any major way.

A great quote from a well known magazine publisher called Malcolm Forbes in 1972 was "you can easily judge the character of a man by how he treats those who can do nothing for him"

How do you treat the cleaner, the waiter in the restaurant?

Is it different to how you treat your boss?

Do you give them less respect?

I have found that people who treat who they think are the "little people" badly, it's to try to make themselves look "bigger", because they have so little confidence themselves.

Treat everyone, whomever you meet, as you yourself would like to be treated.

When I was working in the US, the cleaner came in to my office every night to empty my trash bin and I always took some time to speak to him for a few minutes.

Just passing the time of day.

Why would I just ignore him? (I wouldn't ignore anyone else who came in to my office)

I wonder how many other people in their offices stopped for a minute or two to chat to him and find out how his day/life was going?

Most people didn't even make eye contact when they passed him.

If I asked almost everyone in the office what the name of the cleaner was I can bet they wouldn't know.

Yet this was someone they saw every single day.

But he was practically invisible to them.

God forbid, but if the building was burning down, and that

cleaner was in the right place to help just one person on the floor to survive, who do you think he might have chosen?

It's nice to be nice.

And if my mum was right and it all comes back to you double - double good or double bad - then this is pretty important stuff!

Whether you are the leader of a team of people or you are working for yourself, building what's called *emotional* loyalty amongst friends or colleagues can be incredibly important.

If people just do stuff because they *have* to, or because you tell them to, how much effort do you think they will put into it?

Do you think they will give it their all, 110%?

How much effort do you think they would put in if they *wanted* to do something (rather than *had* to do something)?

A lot more is the answer for sure.

I have always tried to build emotional loyalty with my teams.

And as I have moved across the globe for different roles, people I worked with before in other markets have picked up their families and their lives and have followed me to the next challenge.

And how much do you think it helps me to know that I have this hard-working loyal team who always have my back?

A huge amount is the answer.

So how do I build this emotional loyalty?

There are three very simple things that I always do.

Firstly, always treat people the same way as I would want to be treated myself.

Next, always treat everyone as equal human beings, no matter what role they are doing.

We all have important jobs to do.

No-one is more important than anyone else.

But equally, no one else is more important than you.

And finally, care about how people feel.

Really care.

Ask them.

And then listen to the answer.

I start my weekly team meetings by going round the table and getting everyone to tell the group how they are feeling.

Not which projects they are working on.

But how they are actually *feeling*.

If someone says they are feeling tired because their child was up sick all night, then we won't think they are simply in a bit of a bad mood that day when they are quiet.

If someone says they are feeling worried as a family

member is having surgery, then we know they don't mean it if they are a bit snappy or pre-occupied that day.

Asking about and caring about how people feel is such an easy way to build emotional loyalty amongst groups of people.

My final point on "it's nice to be nice" is about helping and supporting those who are just starting out.

I remember hearing a great story about Kriss Akabusi MBE, an athlete who has won numerous medals at Olympic Games and World Championships.

Kriss didn't have the easiest start in life and had been in care for 12 years.

He left school with no sense of direction and no real hope.

At 16, Kriss joined the army and was quickly taken under the wing of Sergeant Ian MacKenzie who saw the potential in him and made him feel a real sense of purpose.

Sergeant MacKenzie was an inspiring role model for Kriss.

He encouraged him and helped nurture his talent for sport.

Today Kriss is involved in a project to help young people turn their lives around.

And guess what he calls this initiative?

He calls it "Project Mackenzie" after the sergeant who first inspired and mentored him.

Think about it, who is or has been **your** Sergeant MacKenzie?

Who can you go to for inspiration or advice?

If you don't have anyone now, who **could** you go to?

Who could be your Sergeant MacKenzie.

But even more importantly, whose Sergeant MacKenzie are you?

It's nice to be nice.

# 5 WHAT WILL YOU BE FAMOUS FOR?

When I wore the wrong colour of blazer I totally stood out.

You might say for all the wrong reasons.

But I would say that's not the case.

Because I told everyone I had actually <u>chosen</u> that colour of blazer.

Rather than being a sheep and just simply going with the updated blazer colour like everyone else.

The impression I gave was that I had reviewed the old blazer and the new blazer, and then decided that I preferred the old colour better.

And that was why I as wearing it.

So I was seen as a free thinker.

A big thinker.

I didn't simply follow the crowd.

You could say it sort of made me famous.

For the *right* reasons.

In life, you have to work out what you will be famous for.

And I don't mean famous like getting yourself on a reality tv show kind of famous.

If you run naked through your office or through the hospital ward you work on, or if you turn up at the building site naked, you will certainly get yourself well known.

But that would make you infamous, not famous.

I am talking about being famous and standing out from the crowd for the right reasons.

If you are a builder, just take a look at the classified ads at the back of the local newspaper and you will see how many people are offering the same kind of service as you.

Why should clients pick you over anyone else?

Well, if you were famous for doing a better job than anyone else, that might help.

Or if you were famous for finishing quicker than anyone else, that would be good.

If you were famous for your cheery disposition, that would be great.

If you were famous for singing all day while you were working, that would make you stand out.

But you have to do something more, something more than you are being paid for, to really stand out from the crowd.

To really make sure that your customers can't help tell

everyone about you.

Word of mouth is the most important method of spreading the word about the services you offer.

Word of mouth is the best way for your boss to hear about how great you are.

For example, if you were a builder and you always did all of the above in terms of an excellent job at a competitive price and with the right attitude, that's all well and good.

More than well and good.

Really good in fact.

But if you ended up charging less than your quote because you got finished earlier, then wow.

Do you think that might get your client talking about you to all their friends?

Have you ever heard of a builder doing that before.

I haven't.

That would definitely make you stand out from the crowd.

And word-of-mouth is the best way to grow any business.

People trust people like themselves way more than they trust any messages in advertising.

And that's their friends, their families, their neighbours.

If you do something that gets people talking about you (in a *good* way) that could get you more work than fifty advertisements in the local paper.

And it's free too.

Or imagine if you were known as the builder that always brought along little building toys for the children of the home you were working on.

It sounds crazy I know, but can you think what sort of impact that would have?

It would cost you a tiny amount of money.

A few plastic builder trucks.

But if you said to the home-owner that you thought it would make the building project more fun for their children, to help them understand what was going on.

That you know how disruptive building projects can be and you thought this might help occupy the kids.

Even better if you stuck a small sticker with your company name on the side of the truck.

Anyone who has had a building project done while still living in their house, knows just how stressful that can be.

So if your builder turned up with builder toys for the kids AND he did the project really well, on time (even better, early), and with a big smile on his face, wouldn't that make them stand out from the crowd?

It sure would in my experience.

I read recently about builders in Manchester who left a 'pay packet' for the six year old boy who lived in the house where they had just laid a new patio.

Apparently, the boy had loved going out every day to 'help'

the builders.

And, rather than finding this a hindrance, the builders then left a £10 pay packet for the boy, and it absolutely made this six-year-old's day!

The boy's mum shared the story on social media and it went viral.

What do you think will result in that builder getting more work – another classified ad in the local paper or this kind gesture of the £10 pay packet?

If you were opening a brand new hair salon and, let's say, you have *no* budget for any local advertising.

None whatsoever.

So not even a press advertisement.

If the first weekend you were open you put a poster in your window saying "FREE HAIRCUTS/FREE HAIR COLOUR", do you think that might make people come in?

I mean FREE haircuts.

Whoever has heard of that.

So then they all come in, after they have text everyone they know who might also want to take advantage of this great offer.

And then you do a fabulous haircut.

You really listen to what they want.

You smile and are terrifically happy.

You have bowls of sweets for them and their families.

Do you think that would make you different from any other hairdressers?

There is absolutely no point in you being the same old hairdressing salon as everyone else.

That might keep you ticking over.

But if you are reading this book then you want to do more than tick over.

You want to be the most famous and talked about salon in your town.

Do you think your customers might be more likely to come back if you offered service like I described above?

Do you think you might be building some emotional loyalty as they feel you did them a great haircut, charged them nothing and you were still smiling?

Do you think then they would feel some loyalty towards you and think you deserved their custom next time?

Do you think they might tell their friends and family about this amazing new hairdresser in town?

Or do you think a small ad at the back of the local newspaper, would work better.

I know what I would choose.

Every time.

Think about how many advertisements you see every day of your life.

From ads in the back of newspapers, to ads in magazines,

on the radio, online...everywhere.

Apparently we are all exposed to about 1,000 ads per day.

How many can you remember from yesterday?

Like, really remember.

Remembering the company, the product, what it was selling you, how to contact them.

I would imagine your answer is either none or, if you are very lucky, a couple at most.

It's SO important to stand out from the crowd.

Especially in a small business - who can afford to have advertising that no-one remembers?

You have to stand out and you have to have your "thing" that makes you different, that you are famous for.

I have been thinking a lot about what my "thing" will be to help "Win Your Lottery" become famous.

One idea could be that every time I am interviewed about this book, I buy a lottery ticket for the next draw.

And I give the ticket to the interviewer.

I give away the chance to win millions.

Because there really is no chance.

(well, a teeny tiny one, but not really)

This will show how much I believe in the "Win <u>Your</u> Lottery" ethos.

And it's also something very different.

How many other people will have given the interviewer a lottery ticket.

None.

So it makes me stand out from the crowd.

Giving away lottery tickets becomes my "thing" that I am famous for.

That gets people talking.

And remembering.

It dramatises the book and helps people remember the book.

Another great thing to become famous for is doing more than you are getting paid for now, giving more than you are getting paid for now.

And eventually you <u>will</u> be paid more.

No matter where you are in life or what job you are doing, work out what you can do better than everyone else.

It could be an actual "thing" you do or it could be an attitudinal thing.

I would say that I am famous for being an overwhelmingly positive, can-do person.

You know when you see people in the morning and they always ask just in passing "hi, how are you?" and the standard answer is "oh, not too bad" or "surviving" most of the time.

Well, if you ask anyone what my answer always is to that question, they would all know that I say "never better"

Whenever anyone asks me how I am, I *always* say "never better"

Even if I am feeling a little tired or under-the-weather, this is always my answer when someone asks me this when they pass me in the corridor.

And I say it with a big smile.

Who wants to work with grumpy people?

And when you ask someone how they are when you pass them in the corridor, are you really looking for any detail.

Or are you simply being polite.

I would say it's mostly just being polite, as haven't you already passed the person by the time you hear the answer most of the time.

99.9% of everyone you pass will answer with "fine" or "not too bad" or "ok thanks"

So do you think I will stand out from the crowd when I answer "never better"?

Absolutely I do.

It actually stops people in their tracks!

"Never better," they ask?

"Wow".

Someone from work said to me recently, "Sharry – if you are 'never better' every day, then that means your life must be getting incrementally better every single day."

"That's right," I replied.

"I want to live in your head," he laughed.

Well, he could if he chose to!

I definitely stand out as one of the most positive people in the building.

My motto is "the answer is yes, now what was the question" because I always find a way.

And who doesn't want to work with someone sunny and positive, rather than someone who moans all day.

Work out what you can be famous for and then go all out to achieve it.

Famous for always finishing work on time.

Famous for taking a shorter lunch break.

Famous for always asking for more work as you have finished what you are working on.

Famous for sharing all your knowledge.

Famous for helping people.

Famous for always smiling and walking with your head held high.

If you are not doing this now, then start.

Change your attitude and what you do.

Be the person you want to be.

If you are not sure who or what you want to be, then do what I do when I am looking for answers.

Think of someone you really admire.

It can be a famous person or it can be someone you work with.

See yourself having a conversation with this person.

Imagine the room and all the settings.

See it all in your mind in colour (as thinking in colour means you are using your imaginative side of the brain)

Now ask the person what they were famous for?

Ask them for advice for you.

As them what you could be famous for in your industry.

And then set about making yourself famous for this thing.

As then it will be your "thing".

Do it before someone else does.

It can sometimes feel daunting, doing something that you know will make you stand out from the crowd.

For some people, they would much rather "fit in" and be a face in the crowd.

But that's not the way to get on and to win your own lottery.

That's for those who are happy with a more mediocre existence.

I remember years ago watching the TV show Big Brother when it first came out.

If you have never seen it, it involves a group of contestants who live in a house together under constant surveillance.

Members of the public vote for which contestant *they want to evict* each week, until there is an eventual winner.

In Big Brother, there are always the really controversial contestants.

The ones who most polarize the viewing public.

They are the ones who get the ratings up though, as everyone wants to watch them and see what they do.

They keep things interesting.

And then there are the quiet (boring?) contestants who are happy to sit quietly in the background.

My problem with the format of the show was that the most interesting housemates were often voted out first.

They were the ones that everyone had an opinion on.

They were the ones that had the public talking - either because they loved them or because they hated them.

The quieter contestants were not talked about.

And therefore they didn't attract any eviction votes.

The interesting contestants were often the ones voted out first which left for a very boring group of housemates to watch in my opinion.

I always switched off halfway through the series.

It's a bit like in business.

There are employees who are happy just to sit and go along with the status quo.

They go with the flow and don't think of radical new ideas or ventures for the organization.

The employees who are the most passionate, the most engaged - they are the ones coming up with all the new ideas.

Now the only thing with coming up with new ideas is that not everyone will like them.

There will be lots of criticism as the ideas are thrown around and then worked in detail.

And many times the ideas will be rejected.

And that just means you should come up with more/different *new* ideas.

Better ideas.

But imagine if everyone was just like these quiet contestants.

The business would have no new ideas and would eventually just become dated and irrelevant.

Just like when people like me switched off halfway through the series when it got boring.

If you work in a team, don't be afraid to suggest new ways of doing stuff.

Yes there's a risk that not everyone will like them.

And you are definitely opening yourself up to criticism.

But much better that than being passive and, eventually, irrelevant yourself.

I have always found that, if you stand for something – some people will stand with you, and some people will stand against you.

But if you don't stand for something, then no-one will stand with you.

Don't be afraid to put your head above the parapet.

Putting your head above the parapet won't be for everyone, but I am presuming you are reading this book as you want much more from life.

It can be a bit nerve-wracking to do or say things you haven't done before and there's an amazing technique I came across when you are about to enter into things that may seem a little daunting.

It might help and it's really super simple.

I remember when I was doing a big presentation for the first time to hundreds of people, including my boss's boss's boss.

I was really nervous, but I had put myself forward for it as I wanted to stand out from my peers.

There was a big conference coming up and I volunteered to speak on a certain subject.

I knew my stuff and I knew that no-one else at my level would be speaking at the conference.

All the other speakers were much more senior than me.

As the presentation date came closer I got more and more nervous.

Like I said earlier though, I spent a lot of my spare time reading about famous and successful people from all walks of life and what helped them

And I was reading about something that the incredible boxer Muhammad Ali used to do before he went in to the ring.

Before every fight, he created in his mind what he called his "future history"

By this he meant picturing himself going through the whole fight in his mind – every round.

And he pictured himself at the end of the fight, with the referee saying he had won.

He would see himself with his arms in the air.

He would smell the smells.

Hear the roar of the crowd.

Imagine it so vividly it was as though it were really happening.

So when he walked into the ring, in effect it was much easier for him because he had already fought this opponent before.

And he won.

So his subconscious mind believed he actually had fought

this opponent before.

And beat him.

When you do anything for the second time it's always much easier right.

Just like riding a bike.

And in his mind, he had already fought this exact fight before.

And come out victorious.

So all he had to do was do it all again.

It's a method I used before this big presentation.

I saw myself walking into the auditorium.

I saw the crowds.

I heard the rustle of their papers.

I pictured their faces.

I visualized their amazement at what I was saying.

I totally exaggerated in my mind how much they were loving what I was saying.

I saw them hanging on my every word.

By the end of my presentation they were all on their feet, laughing and cheering.

The applause was deafening.

I even pictured my boss's boss's boss coming up to the stage and giving me a high five!

That's how much he loved the presentation.

On the day of the presentation, I kept going over this again and again in my mind.

I visualized myself giving the presentation and then saw the same over-exaggerated reaction at the end.

So by the time I walked on the stage, I had actually delivered this presentation many times before.

And each time, the crowd didn't just like it, they loved it!

I cannot tell you how much this simple process works.

I was so relaxed when I walked on that stage.

And I know I delivered my presentation eloquently and without nerves.

At the end of my presentation on the day, there was a Question & Answer session with the speakers and I actually shared with the audience how I had been feeling and the technique I had used.

I even shared that I had seen the big boss high-fiving me.

And do you know what he then did?

He came up on stage and he *did* high-five me!

Talk about creating an accurate future history.

Talk about you get whatever you think about.

I definitely became famous after doing that presentation.

So push yourself.

Be famous.

Stand out from the crowd like you have worn the wrong colour of blazer amongst a crowd who all look the same.

I promise you will never look back.

Don't look back unless you want to go that way.

Don't follow the crowd.

Or you'll get lost in the crowd.

Stand out and be famous.

(But remember, not infamous).

# 6 YOU HAVE TO HAVE SELF-DISCIPLINE

As a child, I developed a habit of biting my nails.

It started when I overheard some girls talking about me on a bus and saying my chin stuck out.

They were laughing at me.

In fact, they said I had a "witch's chin"

Now up until that point I had never really given my chin very much thought.

But after that I thought about it all day long - about how I had a "witch's chin"

And by the time I went home at night and looked in the mirror at my chin...well, we have all read the previous chapters about the power of the mind, so you can guess what I saw when I looked in the mirror.

That's right.

In my mind, I actually did now have a witch's chin.

And it looked just awful.

Yikes, I had to do something about this.

I had to make sure no-one else could see this witch's chin that I had.

But it was right there on my face.

How could I cover it up?

And then I thought of it.

I had the answer to my problem.

And so that day, I started biting my nails.

As when I was biting my nails, one of my hands was always covering up my chin.

So no-one would be able to see whether my chin stuck out or not.

Brilliant.

As I got older, I realized it didn't matter what these girls or anyone else for that matter thought or said.

And while I am certainly no supermodel, I guess I looked ok.

Yes, I was happy enough with how I looked.

But by then the nail-biting habit had stuck as I had been doing it for years.

I really wanted nice nails like all my friends.

I wanted to go for manicures.

Wear different nail varnish to match my outfits.

Be able to tap my nails on a table.

Or even do simple stuff like peel off a label.

Not to have to hide my hands in shame in important meetings or when I went out for dinner.

I was ashamed of my nails.

They made me look like I was a nervous wreck and I really wasn't.

I really, really wanted to have nice nails.

What a disappointment that I didn't have nice nails.

If only I had nice nails.

What a shame that I didn't.

It was such a huge frustration of mine.

I used to be so sad about not having nice nails.

Until I realized how stupid this was.

How stupid I was being.

I was treating it in the same context as if it was "what a shame I am not six feet tall".

As though it was something I had no control over.

I was thinking about this one day and I had a bit of a revelation.

The only thing I had to do to have these nice nails like everyone else was to stop biting my nails.

It was as simple as that.

Stop biting them.

From that moment onwards.

So I wrote down my goal that I had lovely nails.

I visualized myself with lovely nails.

In my mind I saw and I heard people complementing me on my nails.

I also told everyone that I no longer bit my nails.

And I told myself with absolute certainly that I was not a nail-biter.

So I stopped biting my nails.

And a few weeks later I went for a manicure.

I then had nice nails like all the other girls.

Simple as that.

Self-discipline.

Control yourself and your actions.

Don't let your actions control you.

We are a body driven by a brain.

Not a brain driven by a body.

We can control what we do.

We just have to decide to do it and then to stick to it.

Most people actually do *know* what they should do.

They just don't want to do it.

That sounds harsh but I am afraid it's the truth.

I remember one of my bosses talking to the leadership of the company I was working for at the time on what we had to do for the business to be a success.

He was speaking to the entire leadership team.

And he had a four step process to present to us all.

We were all ready and waiting for this amazing insight.

He was a wonderful leader.

We were all sure this was going to be just fantastic.

Life changing indeed.

Number **one** he said was we had to work out where we are now.

And to be truthful about that reality.

Not to try to hide the truth or make it appear better that where we actually were.

*Great start.*

*We all wrote this down.*

Number **two** was to work out where we wanted to go.

What did we want to achieve in the future.

We had to be really clear about our goals, our vision.

*Got that, what next.*

Number **three** was to work out what we had to do to get from where we were now to where we wanted to go.

Work out what were the steps we had to take to achieve our goals and our vision for the company or for our department.

*We were all still writing, but were really waiting, anticipating the punchline.*

*Nothing too surprising so far, the next and last step surely had to be something huge.*

And his number **four**, once we had worked out all the steps we had to take to achieve those goals was....

To take those steps.

Take.

Those.

Steps.

Now this seemed super simple to me and to all of us.

Was that it?

That was the great insight from this great leader.

And it probably does seem super simple and just common sense to anyone else listening to it too.

I remember asking him why this was the secret to the future success for our business.

Asking how could this be a differentiator when it was so simple and so obvious?

And what he said really stopped me in my tracks.

He said that it was such a game changer because *most people stop at step three.*

They know where they are.

They know where they want to be.

They can work out what they have to do to get where they want to be.

But they don't have the self discipline to execute their plan.

To do whatever is necessary to execute the plan and to achieve their results.

To never give up.

To keep going until they achieve their goals.

To get over every hurdle and never give up until the company's vision and objectives have been realized.

Now most people will not like to hear this.

They might completely dismiss this.

But they know deep down that this is true.

I had a friend who was overweight.

Probably around 60 pounds overweight.

She always used to say to me that she was overweight because she had had children.

I hadn't had children at this stage, so I accepted that this was why she was overweight.

One day she told me she went out for lunch with some colleagues in her office.

They were all mothers and yet she was the only one who was overweight.

She looked around the table and looked at herself and she thought to herself "what's wrong with me - I am just as clever as all these other women"

"So why am I overweight and they are not".

And we all know what the answer was.

Because she ate more than them and didn't exercise as much as them.

From that moment onwards, she vowed then to eat less and exercise more and to be like the other mums.

If they could do it, then so could she.

It was as simple as that.

Self discipline.

And she did it.

Admit where you are now (overweight not because you had children, but because you eat too much and don't exercise enough)

Know where you want to be (a more healthy weight range like the other women)

Know what you have to do to get there (eat more healthily and exercise more)

And then do it.

I remember there was a supermodel I always used to admire.

She looked amazing.

I was lucky enough to meet her in real life as she was also a successful businesswomen.

And in real life she looked even more fantastic.

How lucky was she I thought.

How lucky to have such an amazing figure.

But actually luck didn't come into it.

I read an interview with her husband who said he was astounded at what she had to go through to look the way she did.

What she had to eat.

And how often she had to exercise.

How early she got up in the morning so she could exercise, look after their baby (yes, she still had a terrific figure after having a baby) and run her business.

But it wasn't luck was it.

It was sheer hard work and determination.

Someone told me recently that I was lucky.

Lucky to live in the house I live in.

Lucky to be able to go on nice holidays.

Lucky to have a nice new car.

Lucky to have a swimming pool

I agreed with them.

I *am* lucky.

But I also told them that the hardier I worked, the luckier I got.

I spell luck like this:

H.A.R.D.  W.O.R.K.

Do what you have to do to achieve your goals.

Successful people pay the price.

Either sit on the sofa, or work towards your goal.

When I was writing this book it was summer in Florida (summer in Florida is about March to November by the way)

I was working extremely long hours at work.

I have two children who were under ten at the time.

I would much, much rather be in the pool with the kids or at the beach.

But instead I sat at home typing out page after page.

When I got home from work about 8pm each night I would spend about an hour with the kids, speak to my husband for about half an hour and then I would get started on the book again.

No TV.

No extra time in bed looking at Instagram.

Just getting straight to it.

Doing whatever was necessary to get my book finished.

Because all the time I thought what if someone else does it before me?

What if someone else brings out a positive thinking/power of the mind book that instead of having clever words and complicated theories, instead used simple words and understandable tips that were simple to grasp.

I had to do whatever was necessary to get my book finished.

Before anyone else did.

It's amazing how many people fail at step four.

They know what they have to do to get to where they want to get to - but they just can't be bothered doing it.

They simply choose not to put all the effort in.

Have you ever had a brilliant idea, but you did nothing about it.

And then years later you see someone else has implemented your idea.

Hey, this was your idea.

Why have they stolen it?

But they haven't stolen it, have they.

It *was* a good idea.

They just committed to do whatever was necessary to make it happen.

Before you did.

Have you ever heard the saying that the definition of madness it to keep doing the same thing over and over again and yet expecting different results?

Well unless you do things differently or change your stuff, your results will just stay exactly the same and your life won't move forward from where you are now.

Make a choice.

Made a decision.

And then stick to it.

It will take time so you have to keep at it.

You can't plant a tomato seed tomorrow and then expect to be eating a nice tomato salad the next weekend.

You have to keep going.

If you want more from life and if you want more than you have right now, then you have to do more.

No-one will hand it to you on a plate.

And because 99.9% of people are not willing to do more, you have a really good chance of success.

You are in a minority.

This is so simple, but it's like the world's best kept secret.

The diet industry makes a fortune from different diet

plans.

But all we have to do is to not eat the cake and instead get off the sofa and move around.

This is not rocket science.

It's self discipline.

What do you want more - to eat the cake in about sixty seconds?

Or to wear your favourite dress that has been in the back of your wardrobe for months or years because you couldn't fit into it any more?

Which one will make you feel happier in the long term?

It can be the same with money.

How many people live from pay check to pay check?

Literally running out of money a few days or even a week or more before they next get paid.

Apparently millions of people in the UK are one pay check away from losing their homes as they couldn't pay the rent.

I would challenge you to save money.

As little as ten pounds a month if that's all you can afford.

That's just over two pounds a week.

Most people could save two pounds a week.

There's something about seeing money accumulating in your bank account that makes you want to keep adding to it.

It's a bit like when you start to lose weight and get fitter.

Once you start seeing results, you feel motivated to keep going.

Use the money that you save to help you move towards your goal.

And only use it to help you move towards your goal.

Take a course.

Buy a book.

Go to a conference.

Buy an audio course.

Every spare penny on helping you achieve your goal.

Another very powerful thing that stops us achieving our goals in this big black box in the corner of most of our living rooms or the little black box we hold in the palms of our hands.

The television and the phone.

Stop watching tv.

And stop spending every spare minute on social media.

When you have achieved your goals you can sit and watch tv again (for a limited time) but right now that is wasted time.

Stop listening to the radio on your way to work.

Instead, listen to an audio course that will help you move towards your goal.

I agree it's not as much fun right.

When I was writing this book when I was living in Florida, it was the build up to the American elections (the one where Donald Trump won) and it was completely fascinating.

I would have loved to listen to and watch CNN for hours each day to see what Donald Trump and Hilary Clinton were saying about each other.

But if I did that I wouldn't be moving towards my goal.

So I instead spent all my spare time at home writing my book and my spare time in the car thinking about my book.

There are so many books about time management.

But really we can't manage time.

We can't stop it, or slow it down.

All we can do is control **what we do** with the time we have.

Think about what you spend your time on?

How many people say, I have no time to exercise.

I have no time to think about and write down my goals.

I have no time to read books or to listen to audio courses.

I would suggest that you haven't got time not to.

Work out how you spend your time now and work out those things that don't actually help you move forward with your life.

Stop doing those things and instead do the things that **will** move you towards your goals.

And do it now.

For all of your goals, write out your simple four step process.

1. Where you are now

2. Where you want to be

3. What are all the steps you have to take to get there

4. Commit to taking those steps

And of course, vow never to give up until you get there.

Never, ever give up.

Without this process, goals are only dreams.

I knew that I wanted nice nails.

I was ashamed on how my hands looked.

I knew what I had to do to have nice nails.

But not until I committed to step four did I achieve my goal.

It really is that simple.

I didn't say it was easy.

But it is simple.

Self-discipline.

Discipline yourself.

# 7 IF IT'S TO BE, IT'S UP TO ME

When we were living in Florida, we were more popular than ever before with people wanting to come and visit us.

One year my family visited us over Thanksgiving.

Both my children have birthdays around that time and my family wanted to stay long enough to celebrate both birthdays.

So they stayed for three weeks.

When they were with us my husband and I took full advantage of the live-in babysitters and went out a few times a week for drinks and meals.

And we went out with my family a lot too.

Or had BBQs in the garden.

We had such a lovely time.

And enjoyed a glass of wine or two most evenings.

When they went home, I noticed my clothes seemed a lot tighter.

So I weighed myself.

I was shocked.

I had gained nearly ten pounds in just three weeks.

How could that be?

I was not happy.

So you know what I did.

I blamed my family.

All those delicious meals they cooked for us.

All that entertaining we had to do.

All the empty calories in the additional glasses of wine we were drinking.

If they hadn't been here, I wouldn't have put on all that extra weight.

I was not happy.

Until I realized how stupid I was being.

Did they force feed me?

Of course not.

Did they tell me what I should select off the menu when we went out?

Or did they discourage me from ordering the salads?

Nope, that was me too.

I was way too quick to blame others for something that was

all my doing.

Now how many of us do this?

How many of us blame other people?

Do you ever trip up on basically nothing when you are walking along a pavement and then turn around to see what was to blame?

There must have been a crack in the road.

You must have tripped over something.

It couldn't just be *you*.

There's no way *you* could be to blame.

What's that saying "a bad workman always blames his tools"

I hear so many people blaming their life on their upbringing.

They didn't have great parents.

They grew up in poverty.

Or in a bad area.

They didn't have a chance in life.

It's not their fault they turned out how they did.

Now granted, as a child there's not a whole lot you can do.

But as an adult in your 20s, 30s, 40s, 50s, 60s or even older, your life is your accountability.

No-one else's.

Yours.

So many people feel sorry for themselves.

They think like a victim.

Like they have no control.

Victims like to complain about their life and blame others.

Those in charge of their life don't.

Simple as that.

Decide to stop blaming your past from this day forward.

Take charge.

You can't change a single thing about the past.

But you can change from this exact moment onwards.

I have read so many inspirational stories about people who have overcome huge adversity in life and gone on to become successful.

Let me tell you about a young girl who was born to a single mother on welfare in rural Mississippi.

She was molested throughout her childhood and early teens.

She ran away from home and was pregnant at 14.

Her child, a son, was born prematurely and died in infancy.

Would you agree that this girl had had a challenging start in life - more challenging than most.

And then would it surprise you to learn that I am talking

about Oprah Winfrey, who at one stage was ranked the most influential woman in the whole world.

If Oprah can overcome all of that, can you overcome the challenges in your life?

The answer is, you can.

Of course you can.

But it's up to you.

Let go of the blame or anger you are carrying.

A technique I learned was that if you have a situation that you keep dwelling on, that you are really angry about, picture it like a huge volcano exploding.

Then think of yourself holding on to a piece of lava from the exploding volcano.

Now if you hold onto that piece of lava, you know what's going to happen.

That's right, you are going to get burnt.

So let it go.

Throw it away.

Remember, delete, delete, delete..

Whatever works for you.

Some people use their background or their situation as an excuse to stay exactly where they are now.

To stay in the same rut they are in.

Because they are scared to take risks.

Scared of failure.

Scared to stand out from the crowd.

But at the same time, unhappy with where they are now.

And desperate to win the lottery.

To escape.

To change their life.

If you knew for certain that whatever you were setting out to do or change would be a success, a guaranteed success, what would your goal be?

What would you dare to believe that you could accomplish?

Because most things **are** possible if you just put your mind to it.

How do you think I felt when I started writing this book?

And when I told my children I was writing a book and that it would be published.

(Because remember, telling people about your goal motivates you to achieve it)

I definitely still had a little bit of fear.

In fact a lot of fear.

And sometimes I worried that it wouldn't work.

I might get writers block and not be able to finish it.

I might send it to publishers and no-one would like it.

Even worse, they would laugh at it.

Whoever heard of a book written in this style?

It just wasn't nearly fancy enough.

Wasn't I educated?

Where were all my big words.

This book was just common sense.

Why ever would anyone buy it.

My children would be disappointed in me.

My husband would be supportive, but deep down he would be disappointed too.

I would let everyone down.

What a failure I would be.

Yes, I admit it.

I momentarily would have had thoughts like this.

But then I would put them right out of my mind and get on with it.

I deleted them immediately from my mind.

Over and over again – delete, delete, delete.

And quickly switch out to a positive thought.

I *would* write the book.

I saw myself being a huge success.

I pictured myself on TV doing interviews on the book and how these simple techniques really could change lives.

In fact, I have already imagined me telling the TV interviewers that I had pictured this moment in my mind before.

Me on their show, talking about the book and spreading the word.

(and giving out free lottery tickets!)

And so I got myself back on track.

What are you scared of?

And if you did it anyway, what would be the worst thing that could happen?

Some people say they are simply naturally a pessimist.

Naturally sceptical.

Like it's not their choice and it's definitely not their fault.

I am not sure if I agree.

Maybe they are just scared.

Scared of getting their hopes up.

They say they always expect the worst so then they get a nice surprise if things work out a little better than the worst possible scenario.

Is that really good enough, to settle for just a little bit better than worst case?

Those who decide to give it a go, despite the fear, are

those who are the most successful.

And those who never give up.

Winston Churchill reportedly said "Never, never, never give up".

Remember the phrase "if it first you don't succeed, try, try again"

So keep trying until you *do* succeed.

The story goes that Thomas Edison made over one thousand unsuccessful attempts before he managed to invent the lightbulb.

How many of us would have kept going after ten, twenty, even one hundred attempts?

But he didn't see it as one thousand failed attempts.

He saw each as successful.

Successful in showing him how *not* to invent a lightbulb.

So he kept going.

And he never gave up.

And eventually he worked out how the lightbulb would work.

If you never give up, then you will always get there in the end.

You have to.

We talked a lot about self discipline in the last chapter.

It takes a lot of self discipline not to blame others when things don't work out exactly as you want them to.

And admittedly, some things may be out of your control.

But what you *can* control is your responses.

You are free to choose your responses.

(Remember **response - ability**)

In fact, you are free to choose what you want to do, say, feel or think about a lot of things.

But then you have to accept the results of that choice.

How happy would you say you are right now on a scale of one to ten?

Give yourself a score on how happy you are about your work.

Your relationships.

Your fitness.

Your weight.

Write it out or store in a note on your smart phone.

Now work out what you think would make you happy.

And commit to change.

Commit to doing everything you can to work towards it.

Never, ever giving up.

Being clear on your goals and knowing that you are working towards them helps you feel in control.

You will feel happier and more content if you feel you are heading toward those things that make you happy.

You will feel much more at ease.

Which is so much better than feeling the opposite of being at ease.

Another word for not being at ease, is dis – ease.

The opposite of feeling at ease.

You might recognize this word as disease.

I know what I would prefer.

Everything that I have read and learned points towards those always feeling ill at ease as being much more likely to get ill.

Their immune system is weakened as they have to fight off their internal negative thoughts and dramas that may only exist in their heads.

Instead of fighting off all the cold and flu bugs that *do* actually exist.

Focus on what makes you happy.

It doesn't matter how old you are reading this.

No-one is too old to change.

To change their thoughts.

To change their life.

To feel more at ease.

I worked with a wonderful woman who started learning karate at 75.

She got a job working in a supermarket at 81.

At 95, she got her black belt.

When I worked with her, she was 97.

And still working.

Happily so.

How often do you hear of people who work hard all their lives and then retire and die soon afterwards.

I wonder if it's because they don't have a focus.

A purpose.

A reason for being.

We all need to work towards what makes us happy and put all our energy into it.

Don't ask "why me" when things go wrong.

Ask "why not me" when you are imagining greater things for yourself!

See yourself at your best.

Use the future histories we learned about.

Last thing at night, think about two things.

1.  Mentally list out the best things in your life right now

2.  And read and visualize your goals as though you have already achieved them

You will be amazed just how much energy this gives you.

You know you hear these stories about people who have managed to lift the front of a car off someone who was trapped underneath.

And afterwards they have no idea where they found the strength.

I have a theory.

It could be because they believed it was possible.

Sir Roger Bannister was the first person to run a mile in under four minutes, setting the record at 3 minutes 59.4 seconds on the 6th May 1954.

Runners had apparently been chasing that goal seriously since as far back as the late 1800s.

But Sir Roger's record stood for just 46 days before John Landy, an Australian runner, broke the record again at 3 minutes 57.9 seconds.

Then just a year later, three runners broke the four minute barrier in a single race.

And over the last half century, more than a thousand runners have conquered a barrier that for decades had been thought to be truly out of reach.

Because **they knew that it was possible.**

There's a wonderful story in a brilliant book called "Predatory Thinking" on motivation and the power of the mind by the wonderful UK based advertising genius and best selling author Dave Trott.

It's so good, I have copied it here for you, with Dave's permission.

I also love the fact that it's an example from everyday life in a UK based football team.

And not from the board room.

## MOTIVATION

*Bill Shankly took over as manager of Liverpool when they were in the Second Division.*

*He took a group of players and motivated them to win promotion.*

*He motivated them to fight their way up the First Division (the equivalent of the Premier League).*

*He motivated them to win the First Division.*

*He motivated those players to beat the best in England.*

*Then he motivated them to play against the best in Europe.*

*In 1965 they played in the European Cup against the champions of Germany: FC Cologne.*

*They played in Cologne and they drew.*

*They had the replay in Liverpool and they drew.*

*They had to play a deciding game at a neutral venue.*

*They played in Rotterdam and they drew.*

*Even after extra time they still drew.*

*After 400 minutes of football the game was decided on the toss of a coin, which Liverpool won.*

*The team came back to England and three days later they had to play Chelsea.*

*In the semi-final of the FA Cup.*

*And they were spent.*

*They sat in the dressing room before the Chelsea game, knackered.*

*Shankly stood and looked at the team.*

*He said* **"Lads I've got something here I didn't want to show you in case it upset you. But there's nothing to lose now so I might as well."**

*And he took a brightly coloured brochure out of his pocket and held it up.*

*He said* **"This is the leaflet that Chelsea have had printed for when they get to the final at Wembley.**

**They think it's a formality that they'll win tonight, because they think you're knackered.**

**They think you left everything on the field in Rotterdam.**

**They think flying over there and playing the Germans took it out of you, so they think you're easy meat now.**

**That's why they've printed up their brochure for when they get to Wembley.**

**After the formality of brushing Liverpool aside.**

**What do you think lads, is it a formality?**

**Can they just brush you lot aside?**

**Are you as knackered, as done in as they think?**

**Are you finished?"**

*As he spoke the players began to get irritated, then*

*annoyed, then furious.*

*Chelsea thought they'd just brush Liverpool aside did they?*

*Thought Liverpool would just roll over did they?*

*And Shankly's team went out and ran the legs off Chelsea.*

*Liverpool won two nil and knocked Chelsea out of the FA Cup.*

*After the match Bill Shankly walked over to Chelsea's manager, Tommy Docherty, to shake hands.*

*Docherty was shell-shocked.*

*He said **"Bill, how did they ever manage that? They've just come back from playing against the German champions in Rotterdam? How come they've got so much energy?"***

*And Bill Shankly handed him the Chelsea Cup Final programme.*

*He said **"There you are Tom, a little souvenir."***

*Tommy Docherty looked at it and said **"What the f\*ck's this?"***

*He didn't recognise it.*

*He didn't recognise it because Chelsea hadn't printed it.*

*Bill Shankly had just the one copy printed to show his team before the match.*

*Just to motivate them a little bit*

What an amazing story.

It's incredible what *you* can do if you just put your mind to it.

If you are not sure what will make you happy, then talk to people you see as successful and happy.

If you are a teacher, ask the Head who has been famous for completely turning around an underperforming school.

If you are a nursing student, ask the nurse who seems to love her job and who is the most popular with all the patients.

You will be amazed how happy they will be to share what they know.

Learn from them.

But don't think they are better than you.

They are not better than you.

No-one is better than you.

They just know more.

If you believe someone is worth more.

Then that makes you worth less.

Worthless.

And you are not.

Be decisive.

Hundreds of squirrels are squashed on the middle of our roads as they couldn't decide which way to go when the car came.

No-one else could tell them.

They had to decide.

But they froze paralysed instead.

They did nothing.

And they got squashed.

Don't be a squirrel.

I guarantee you, there are people less qualified than you who are doing the things you wanted to do and who have the things you wanted to have - and all because they believed in themselves and they took action.

Be determined to make the rest of your life, the best of your life.

Believe in yourself.

And remember.

If it's to be, it's up to YOU.

Make a decision.

And be less squirrel.

# 8 CHANGE LIKE YOU HAVE DYED YOUR HAIR PINK

Whenever I have started a new job, in a new country, I always think about how I want people to perceive me.

What do I want them to think about me?

Professional businesswomen?

Kind?

Firm but fair?

Friendly?

Decisive?

I am starting from scratch with these people.

They don't know me from Adam (or Eve).

There's no history between us.

But for most people, a change of jobs to a completely new place where no-one knows you isn't always possible or even appropriate.

So you may worry that if you decide to take on board some of the stuff you have learned in this book, what will other people think?

They will notice you are different right?

And they might ask you about it?

My answer is, so what.

So.

What.

If it's a step in the right direction for you, to help you get on better at work, or earn more new clients or recommendations, then so what.

When you are happier and more successful, who'll be laughing then?

And if you are really taking on board what you have picked up in this book, then actually you will be a much nicer person to be around.

So I can't see anyone complaining about that.

I have mentored many, many people over the years.

From junior team members starting out, to more senior Directors who may have found their careers stalling.

To each and every one of them I give the same piece of advice.

*Change like you have dyed your hair pink.*

Nothing subtle.

People have to notice.

Your clients have to notice.

Your boss has to notice.

You need to really disrupt their thinking and their perception of you.

So commit to it fully.

Really change.

Don't just pretend to change and put on an act.

Be 100% of the best person you can be every day.

Don't falter.

Don't go back to what everyone else is doing.

Make sure you get noticed.

Noticed for all the *right* reasons.

Because you are happier, harder-working, more positive and "can-do" than everyone else around you.

Every second of every day.

Your clients notice.

Your bosses notice.

Your work colleagues notice.

Your family notices.

Everyone notices.

And you keep it up consistently until this is basically your new normal.

A subtle change is not enough if you want to stand out from the crowd.

So you change your behaviour to have the same impact as though you had just dyed your hair pink.

Think about it.——

If you dyed your hair bright pink and went in to your office or place of work, do you think people might notice?

Do you think they might comment?

Do you think it would make you stand out from the crowd?

Of course it would.

But for the wrong reasons.

Stand out for all the *right* reasons.

(But I'd probably suggest keeping your actual hair just as it is)

What's most important here is that you have to really believe in what you are doing.

This has to be the new you.

But it's a better version of you.

A much better version.

And to really ingrain this new, improved you, you have to be this better version *consistently*.

Are you one way at work and another way at home?

I'm not.

I can't put on a false act at work each day and then be a different me at night.

All that acting in different ways at different times would be hard work.

Remembering to act in this way at work and then act in that way at home.

That's hard, and uses up a lot of energy.

Instead, be the best version of yourself *all the time* and then it will become second nature.

When I talking about changing as though you have dyed your hair pink, I am talking about *really genuinely changing*.

And then sticking with it.

The sticking with it and really believing it part is incredibly important.

This has to be the new you.

Not just some act.

Don't <u>pretend</u> to be a better person, a more hard-working, positive person.

Actually <u>be</u> and <u>do</u> all of those things.

This will be much more authentic.

Authentic people always act in the same way, even if they

are the only person present.

They are not kind and caring at work, and then go home and kick-the-cat type of people.

This doesn't mean acting like a robot though.

You can still be you – just the best possible version of you.

Being authentic is really important.

Authentic people show empathy.

They show their feelings and that they care.

They are confident enough to show a vulnerability.

Or ask a question if they don't understand.

I was once on a course through work where the first thing the moderator did was show a picture of his family.

His family was him and his husband.

And their lovely dog.

He said he had been anxious to tell work colleagues he was gay but on this course, on this day, he had decided to share.

I immediately remembered him more than any other presenter leading a course.

I remembered him as being real.

And confident.

He got the attention of everyone in the room.

He stood out from the crowd of all the other presenters on

all the other courses.

Be confident in yourself.

I have found that it's people who have no confidence who pretend to know everything all of the time.

No one knows everything all of the time.

Authentic people say if they don't understand jargon.

They ask for help.

I once had a friend who used to be a secretary, let's call her Jane.

Jane worked really hard and got promoted to being a manager.

Good on her, I thought.

But when Jane became a manager, something funny happened to her.

She started talking funny.

I didn't really understand what she was talking about half the time.

I had never even heard of some of the words or phrases she was using.

She actually sounded ridiculous.

I was her friend, so I asked her why she was now speaking different.

She said it was because she wanted to appear more professional now that she was a manager.

She was reading industry publications and picking up on all the 'hot' terminology she said.

And she started to introduce industry 'buzz words' into her conversations.

And to use lots of industry jargon to show that she really understood this industry.

But no-one understood what Jane was saying.

She actually sounded like a bit of a plonker if I am honest.

Quite the opposite of the impression she was *trying* to give.

I have come across a few more people like that as I have worked in different companies.

They use big words and lots of jargon to make themselves appear more clever than everyone else.

It doesn't work.

It never works.

Even if, as you are listening to them speak, you are thinking "wow – this sounds impressive", by the time they have finished speaking you will actually be thinking "sorry, what was that you just said?"

Don't use jargon.

Speak normal.

There's a much better chance of getting your point across and making sure everyone is clear on what needs to be done.

If you are a team leader, speak normal to your team.

If you are in a team, stop using jargon and don't ever think that using complicated words makes you appear more intelligent than other people.

It doesn't.

And it actually means that there's less chance of you getting the desired outcome from your project or task.

And outcomes are what really matters.

Not fancy words.

Speak normal and be yourself, but the *best* version of yourself.

And don't worry about labels or judgements.

If you have small children, look at how they play and don't care what others think of them.

It's when they grow older they start getting self conscious.

If you want people to follow you, they need to follow YOU.

The real you.

They need to know who you really are.

Like the guy leading the course who started out by telling us about his family.

He was being himself, just a braver, more confident version of himself.

Make sure that people get to know the new, improved you.

If you are going for a job interview, my advice is be yourself, but the best possible version of yourself.

Be yourself, and then you will get the job if it's right for you.

What you mustn't do is struggle to fit in somewhere that really isn't right for you or goes against your values.

Be you.

Don't be afraid to be you.

There are some things never to reveal though.

I think your salary is one of them.

I did once work with a small consultancy firm who had a piece of paper on the fridge in the office with the name of everyone who worked there and what their salary was.

The idea was that if your colleagues knew how much you were earning, you would push yourself to demonstrate to them that you were worth every penny.

I think that might be taking authenticity and openness a bit too far for me!

Another thing probably not to assert on other people would be your religious or political beliefs.

Other than that, I try really hard to be myself.

I have seen some people try so hard and for so long to fit in that they are in danger of forgetting who they really are.

Be authentic or you could look like a phoney.

And then you may wonder why people don't trust you.

As the great Oscar Wilde was reported to have said "Be yourself.  Everyone else is already taken"

Be yourself.

But push yourself to be the best version of yourself you can possibly be.

Every minute of every day.

And you can probably leave the pink hair dye in the store.

# 9 HEALTHY BODY, HEALTHY MIND, HEALTHY RELATIONSHIPS

I am allergic to chocolate.

When I eat chocolate, my allergic reaction is to develop rolls of fat around my middle.

OK, so I am not really allergic.

But I just tell myself I am, whenever I want to shed a few pounds.

I tell myself over and over again that I am allergic to chocolate.

I tell work colleagues it over and over too.

So eventually they stop offering it to me when they open a big box to share round.

And eventually, I pretty much believe it myself.

Fake it until you feel it.

Oh no, my allergy has come back.

I can't have any chocolate for a few months until it goes away again.

It really is incredible how this works.

Everyone wants to have a long and healthy life.

And mostly everyone wants to be a healthy body weight.

But guess what, not everyone wants to eat healthily and exercise!

The diet starts Monday right.

Start it now.

Right now.

Push yourself to do what you might not want to do.

Like getting out of bed earlier to exercise.

Like developing unfortunate allergies to unhealthy foods.

I don't think I have met a single person who doesn't want to get fitter or be healthier.

And if you feel better about yourself, then you have more self respect.

And feeling better about yourself makes it a lot easier to focus on some of the other stuff in this book.

So here's a couple of tips that have worked for me in this area.

Again, it's not rocket science.

Number one is the Weekly Weigh In.

Get your husband/wife/partner/parents/housemates etc to weigh you weekly.

It should be the person closest to you.

And then display the chart of your weight somewhere visible in your house.

Somewhere that you can see it every day.

And somewhere that everyone else who lives in the house can see it every day.

So they will see when you lose weight.

And they will see when you don't.

So you might just be that little bit more motivated to achieve results.

It will make you uncomfortable to have your weight journey publicly on show for all the people you live with, but that will push you on!

At one of my jobs, a few of the team were talking about wanting to lose weight, be a bit healthier.

So I brought in some scales and started a weekly weigh in.

We all had to pay a few dollars to be weighed each week, and at the end of the period, the person who had lost the most (as a percentage) walked away with all the money.

The second tip I have is for when you are dealing with hunger pangs.

No-one likes to feel hungry.

'Drink water" someone once told me.

That will fill you up.

Well guess what, it didn't.

I was still hungry.

So I thought I would try to use the tips I had learned about the power of the mind to see if that could help.

When I have that achy feeling of being hungry, I tell myself that's not hunger.

I am not feeling like that because I am hungry.

In fact, that feeling is your body working off fat.

That's just the feeling you get when your body works off fat.

It sounds like a really silly small thing, but it's incredible the difference.

So instead of dreading the hunger pangs, when I get them now I instead feel a bit happier as I know that's just my body getting rid of some of the excess fat.

And that's what I wanted.

Mind over matter.

Feeling better because I know I am moving in the direction of my goal.

And as a goal seeking missile, that's exactly the direction I feel most conformable in.

It's not just about eating less or eating better.

It's also about moving more.

As I said, none of this is rocket science.

Eat less.

Move more.

Four words that sum up every diet and fitness book.

Everyone has time.

Whether you have a new baby or a new job.

Most people can march on the spot in front of the TV instead of sitting on the sofa.

Most people can take the stairs instead of the lift.

You just have to want to.

Or maybe not 'want' to exactly.

But you have to be committed to doing it.

Whether you like it or not.

We have talked a lot in the book about healthy minds and a bit about healthy bodies, and the other thing I wanted to touch on is the importance of healthy relationships.

We have talked a lot about the importance of your interactions with people you work with.

But how you are at home is equally if not even more important.

Now this is not a book full of relationship advice.

There are other books much better qualified at that.

But here's just a few things you may want to think about.

Firstly, really listen when you are talking with your partner.

Switch off the TV.

Put down your phone.

And listen.

When you have listened, reflect back what you have heard.

"Oh, so what I think you are saying is xxxx xxxxx"

Everyone likes to feel listened to and understood.

Show your partner that you care enough to really listen.

So many people don't listen.

Instead, they are just waiting for an opportunity to speak.

The relationships you have with your children can be probably the most important relationships of all.

What children want is your time.

I read recently on a parents' blog online that children spell love like this:-

T. I. M. E.

Give your time.

And when you give it, really give it.

No phones, no distractions.

How many people go to their graves regretting spending too much time with their children and their family.

Exactly.

Show your children you love them *no matter what.*

You might not like what they do, but you always love them.

Think back to your first memory.

What was it?

Was it good or bad?

A positive or negative experience?

What else can you remember about growing up?

What stands out in your mind?

Now think about what your children will say as the answer to these questions when they are grown up.

Every day you are creating memories.

Try to make sure they are good ones.

In this chapter, I also want to talk about two key behaviours that are often overlooked and can make a huge difference to how others see you and having healthy relationships – and that's saying thank you and saying sorry.

My husband and I had some people around for dinner recently.

Just a casual dinner with some people from work.

A few days letter, one of the men who was there, Marcus, sent a handwritten thank you note.

I couldn't ever remember anyone sending a handwritten

thank you note after a dinner party before.

Most people say nothing.

Some might send a quick text.

But Marcus sent an actual handwritten thank you note.

I remembered that much more than I remembered what type of wine anyone had brought or how much fun they were at dinner.

Marcus went straight into the category that I call "really decent people".

And "decent people" get on.

They just do.

Someone once told me that saying thank you is almost as good as giving your team a raise.

It makes them feel valued.

So remember to say thank you to your workmates.

And I don't just mean throwing around praise generally.

Be specific about what you are saying thank you for.

It's not just bosses saying thank you to their teams by the way.

This works both ways.

In Australia, I was lucky enough to have a coach/mentor that I met every couple of months.

After each session, I would send a little thank you note.

In that note, I thanked them for their time and I talked about what I specifically learned as a result of that one-to-one coaching session.

Even if it's something as simple as your boss approving your holiday request – say thank you.

If you have a job interview, write and say thank you afterwards.

If you get appointed to a new role, write and say thank you to whoever interviewed you.

(Including the Human Resources person who supported your new boss in the interview process).

Saying thank you is a small thing.

But it can make a big difference.

Start doing this now.

Whether you were not taught proper manners as a child or whether you just forget, if you are not thanking people then you could just be damaging your career and your relationships.

Saying sorry is just as important.

In my experience, people who don't say sorry tend to have low self esteem.

They just can't admit that they were wrong.

In my marketing job, as a team, you produce a lot of printed materials.

Press advertisements, leaflets, display boards for stores.

Hundreds and hundreds of items every month.

And sometimes we get it wrong.

Could be the wrong spelling, the wrong product, the wrong price.

I remember a time when we printed the wrong press advertisement in the newspaper.

In fact, not just one newspaper, but six different newspapers.

Across six different states.

All on the same day.

Ouch.

Stores were not very happy as we had advertised the wrong products, some of which were not even stocked in their particular state, and also the wrong prices.

Customers were coming in, expecting to get those prices.

I was in a meeting with my boss when the text message came through to me that we had made a serious mistake with the press advertisements.

I quickly text the guy in my team who ran this area for me.

His text back said it was not his team's fault, they were so busy at the moment and this advertisement had been briefed late by another team.

He was basically saying "it's not my fault" and he was very quick to blame another team.

Not particularly helpful.

When I went back upstairs to the team, the person who worked for him, the more junior marketing team member, came up to me and said "I am really sorry Sharry.

This is completely on me.

I am accountable.

The wrong ad went out.

I have already apologized to the Buying team and we are sending a communication to stores explaining what has happened and what they should tell customers.

I have rebooked advertising for this weekend with the right offers to make sure we communicate the right deals to our customers.

I have also put in place new checks and balances to make sure this never happens again."

Which one do you think was the stronger leader that day?

Which one impressed me most?

Think back to when you last made a serious error at work.

If you are a builder, perhaps someone has called you about a snagging list for an extension you built.

If you are a hairdresser, you might have had someone whose hair turned out *nothing* like the photo reference they brought in.

How would you have reacted?

It's amazing how few people actually say "It's my

accountability.

I am sorry.

Here's how I suggest we fix it.

And here's what I am doing to make sure it never happens again."

Imagine if that's how your builder reacted when you called with your snagging list.

Would you be more likely to book them again and to recommend them – of course you would.

Sorry shouldn't be the hardest word and it really can make the difference to a healthy professional or personal relationship continuing or not.

And it definitely helps quickly take the stress out of some situations.

Healthy relationships and a positive mental attitude are so important to health overall.

It really is incredible the power of the mind on your physical state.

After my blazer experience, where I had gone from being embarrassed about the colour to genuinely preferring my blazer, I became really fascinated about the power of the mind.

Once when I was a teenager, I lay in my bed at night and told myself, over and over again, that my legs were paralysed.

I just wanted to experiment how far I could take this.

So I told my legs they were paralysed and then I literally could not move them.

Oh no.

I would panic.

I actually am paralysed.

What can I do?

And then I realized, I just had to tell them they were not paralysed any more.

So I did.

And then I could move them again.

Now I am not saying of course that anyone with any paralysis can do this.

That would be just plain stupid.

But what I am saying is that we have much more power over our bodies and our health that we could ever imagine.

And I think I realized that at a very early age lying in my bed with 'paralysed' legs.

Have you ever called in sick to work?

I am sure most of us have at some point or another.

Or have you ever had someone call in sick at work and you take their call?

What do you notice about their voice?

Is it all quiet and a bit husky and slow and as though the

person is really talking through extreme pain.

It is like the most pained voice you have ever heard in all of your life.

And then a few minutes into the conversation, when you are perhaps sharing a funny story about something happening at work, do they suddenly perk up, as if by magic.

Do they suddenly talk with a normal voice again.

I am not saying they miraculously feel better, but what I am saying is that you can talk yourself into feeling a lot worse.

Don't do it.

Don't make yourself feel worse than you actually are.

So many people have told me when they have been really busy at work and have been working incredibly hard and then they go on holiday and on the first day of the holiday, guess what?

They get a cold.

A stinking cold.

Why is this?

And why does it happen when you are not even going to a different location or a different country with different germs.

I wonder if it's because when we are at work we are driven.

Focused.

We have goals driving us.

Stuff to do every day.

We are too busy to get a cold.

We tell ourselves that for sure.

We can't get ill and have time off work.

There's no way we are getting a cold.

We have no time for a cold.

When we are on holiday, we breathe a big huge sigh of relief.

We have no goals.

No focus.

Nothing driving us.

So we let down our guard and the cold and flu bugs come flying in!

Imagine instead if you had really strong personal goals.

And every day on holiday, you woke up reading about your personal goals and feeling motivated by them.

I wonder if that would make a difference.

I just wonder.

Because just as having a healthy body helps you have a healthy mind, having a healthy mind can also relieve stress levels and help us have a healthy body.

There has been a lot of different stuff in this chapter, from how to improve your physical as well as mental health and fitness, to how to strengthen your personal and professional relationships.

Thinking differently has changed every aspect of my life and it could work for you too.

# 10 THE HEALTHY THINKING DIET

We are coming to the end of this short book and hopefully there are some things in here that will work for you.

What I am asking now, of each and every one of you, is for you to commit to this for just one month.

What's a month after all.

Not a lot in the whole scheme of things.

Just as you may be used to going on a healthy eating diet for a month, I am asking you to go on a *healthy thinking* diet for a month.

Just try it.

What have you got to lose?

And you may find that you want to keep going and keep going as a completely new way of life.

It worked for me and now I have a life I can hardly believe.

If what you focus on most in life you end up getting in your life, then don't you think it's about time you started focusing on the right stuff?

The best way to get something done is to start.

So start right now.

See how long you can go without having a single negative thought.

And whenever a negative thought pops into your mind, see yourself deleting it, the same way as you delete unwanted emails.

Negative thought comes into your mind?

Delete.

Delete.

Delete.

And keep on deleting until you replace it with a positive one.

Imagine that everything you think about you *are* going to get in your life in the future.

Whether you truly believe this to be true or not, if there's just the slightest chance, isn't that a bit scary?

Even if you are sceptical about it, focus on what you *do* want just incase!

And delete, delete, delete all those negative thoughts.

Also in this month, make sure you use your time the best you possibly can.

In business, there's a term called 'Return on Capital',

which is basically how much money you get back from the investment you are putting in to a business.

I like to talk about Return on Time.

If you use your time effectively you will get a great return in terms of your health or your career.

But if you waste time you will stay exactly as you are.

And I am guessing you are reading this book as you don't want to stay exactly where you are.

Make sure you get the best possible Return on Time.

Switch off the TV.

Switch off the radio.

Read more self improvement books.

Listen to an audio course.

Write out your goals and your action plan.

Speak to those currently succeeding in your field.

Or your Return on Time will be a load of old R.O.T.

If success in your career is genuinely important to you, then why watch TV for hours on end.

This sounds tough, but just try if for one month and see if it makes a difference.

These days, everyone seems to want their fifteen minutes of fame, but are not truly prepared to put in their fifteen minutes of pain for the gain!

Also during this month, admit the truth to yourself.

You are not big boned.

You are simply eating more calories than you are burning off.

You are not just a naturally pessimistic person.

No, what you actually are is maybe just a little bit scared.

You are not so busy that you have no time to exercise.

Go on, admit it to yourself.

You would just prefer to have longer in bed or to sit and watch that TV show.

Look around you.

Is there really no-one in the whole wide world with the same type of job and the same family commitments to you who is in better health than you?

Thought so.

Admit the truth of where you are now.

And it doesn't matter where you are.

The past is something you cannot change.

But you can change the future.

Within the month, things will go wrong for sure.

But you will bounceback if you are determined never to give up.

Winston Churchill famously said "If you're going through

hell, keep going"

What brilliant advice.

If you were going through the actual burning hot misery that was actual hell, why would you want to stop there and stay there.

Of course you wouldn't.

You would do what you could to get out of there as soon as you possibly could.

Churchill also said "Success is the ability to go from one failure to another with no loss of enthusiasm"

Keep going.

Never give up.

Never, never, ever give up.

Martin Luther King Jr said "If you can't fly, then run. If you can't run, then walk. If you can't walk, then crawl, but whatever you do, you have to keep moving forward."

We have one life.

Let's live it the very best we can.

Are you really giving 100% to all aspects of your life right now?

Do you think you could do it for just one month?

Try it and see.

Imagine that video recorder or your shoulder.

You will be amazed at the difference you will feel.

And it might just help you win the lottery.

Your **own** lottery.

And who cares what other negative people think.

Who cares if someone doesn't like the colour of your blazer.

## Quick Recap Summary

### 1. Going the extra mile

Act every day like there's a video camera on your shoulder and a million dollar prize up for grabs.

Getting on is 90% attitude; 10% ability.

There is very little difference in people. But the little difference is their attitude. And it can make a BIG difference whether it's positive or negative.

Be a radiator, not a drain.

### 2. You have got to have goals

Don't be a sailboat with no destination - life is too stormy for that.

You have got to have goals and you have to have them written down.

And written down as though they are already true.

Visualize your goals every day.

Tell everyone about your goals - it will motivate you to achieve them.

Become a goal seeking missile every day.

## 3. Happy talk.

Always remember you have a response-ability – you can choose your attitude.

Fake it until you feel it.  Say it over and over to yourself *("I actually prefer this colour")* until you start to actually believe it.

Remember we wake up each day with a full battery and every negative thought depletes some of the energy.  When negative thoughts pop into your head, press delete, delete, delete until a happy one comes along – just as you would delete unwanted emails.

If what you think about is what you get, then make sure you are thinking about the right stuff!

Whether you think you can do something, or whether you think you can't – you are absolutely right.

Whistle while you work.  Remember my good old grandad whistling his way down the coal mines each day.  If the Happiness Advantage is true, then choose to be happy.

## 4. It's nice to be nice

If *"whatever you give out in life you get back double"* is true, you better make sure you give out good.

Treat everyone fairly and equally and never burn any bridges – you never know where people might pop up (remember the interviewee who stole the parking space).

Remember that you are not better than anyone else – but

equally, no-one else is better than you.

Build *emotional* loyalty, so people around you want to go the extra mile for you.

Who inspires you – who is your Sergeant MacKenzie. And just as importantly, whose Sergeant MacKenzie are you.

## 5. What will you be famous for?

You have to be famous for something – you have to stand out from the crowd.

Little things can make a big difference – remember the builder who gave his client's son a £10 pay packet.

You have to have your 'thing'. Mine was "never better" and a can-do attitude ("the answer is yes, now what was the question"). What's yours going to be.

And if it feels awkward to stand out from the crowd, create your own 'future histories' until you feel comfortable.

## 6. You have to have self-discipline

Admit truthfully where you are now.

Work out where you want to go.

Unlike the advice in some other books, it's not enough to simply put these dreams and goals out there into the universe. You have to work out a plan for what you need to do to get yourself there.

And then you have to execute that plan. You have to be

prepared to do **whatever is necessary** to achieve your goal.

Don't stop until you have completed step 4. Never give up. Never ever give up.

If you want more than you have now, then you need to do more than you are doing now.

Remember, we can't control time – but we can control what we do with the time that we have.

## 7. If it's to be, it's up to me

Stop blaming other people- if you hold on to anger, it's like holding on to a piece of hot lava from a volcano – you're the one who is going to get burnt.

If you think you *can* do something or if you think you *can't* do something, then you are absolutely right.

How bold would your goals and ambitions be if you knew for sure that you were going to be successful in achieving them. Believe in yourself. Back yourself. Remember how quickly Roger Bannister's record was broken when people believed it was possible.

You feel at ease to the same extent as you feel in control of your life. Take control. Only you can do it.

Make a decision and take action – be less squirrel.

## 8. Change like you have dyed your hair pink

Commit to changing 100%. Give it everything you have and stand out for all the right reasons.

Don't make half-hearted attempts. Make sure everyone notices your change.

But **really** change, consistently. Don't just put on an act some of the time.

Remember, using fancy words and jargon does not make you look good – speak normally and just be yourself, but the best possible version of yourself.

Don't be embarrassed – remember, no-one will be laughing when you are happier and more successful than ever.

## 9. Healthy body, health mind, healthy relationships.

Commit to a healthier lifestyle – what are you now allergic to?

Be mentally present for your family when you are physically present – remember that children spell love T.I.M.E.

Remember the power of manners – say thank you. And step up when you get it wrong and say sorry – it really can take the stress right out of situations.

A healthy body helps you have a healthy mind. And the reverse is also true – a healthy mind helps you achieve a healthy body.

## 10.    The healthy thinking diet.

You have probably all been on a healthy eating diet - well now try the healthy **thinking** diet.

Try it for a month.  Starting right now.

No matter how tough things are now - stay focused and stay with this.  Remember "if you are going through hell, keep going".

What have you got to lose.  Try it for a month.

It might just help you win the lottery.  Your own lottery. The lottery of life.

## A Favour?

I have a small favour to ask.

And if you believe that whatever you give out in life you get back double, then hopefully you will all be happy to help!

If you liked what you read in this book, would you mind awfully leaving a positive review on Amazon.

It honestly makes a huge difference and I would be so grateful.

And please do follow me on twitter @winyourlottery.

Thanks again for buying my book.

I truly hope it helps you win the lottery, your own lottery, the lottery of life.

# ABOUT THE AUTHOR

Sharry Cramond has worked all over the world as a marketing executive and this is her first book. She has always been passionate about inspiring others on the power of positivity and she wrote this book after Kelly Wallace, who worked for CNN at the time, told her she should after hearing Sharry talk at a conference in the US. Sharry lives in Hertfordshire in the UK with her husband and their two children.

Printed in Poland
by Amazon Fulfillment
Poland Sp. z o.o., Wrocław